TUNE-UP YOUR RELATIONSHIP

Barbara Rice & Andrew Rice

Copyright © 2020 Barbara Rice & Andrew Rice

All rights reserved

The characters and events portrayed in this book are fictitious. Any similarity to real persons, living or dead, is coincidental and not intended by the author.

No part of this book may be reproduced, or stored in a retrieval system, or transmitted in any form or by any means, electronic, mechanical, photocopying, recording, or otherwise, without express written permission of the publisher.

ISBN-13: 9780578749945
ISBN-10: 0578749947

Cover design by:Fiverr #142
Library of Congress Control Number: 2018675309
Printed in the United States of America

Unless otherwise indicated, Scripture quotations are from the Holy Bible, New International Version, copyright 1973, 1978, 1984 by the International Bible Society. Used by permission of Zondervan Bible Publishers.

Most of the people described in this book have had their names and identifying characteristics changed for confidentiality. The exception to this is those I get to brag about.

CONTENTS

Title Page	1
Copyright	2
Chapter One: The Art of Listening	7
Chapter Two: The Art of Speaking	22
Chapter Three: Annoying Anger	36
Chapter Four: Giving Forgiveness	50
Chapter Five: Resolving Conflict	64
Chapter Six: Problem Solved!	78
Chapter Seven: Admiring Each Other's Differences	93
Chapter Eight: Cultivating Intimacy	108
Chapter Nine: Goals and Beyond	123
Congratulations!	138
Why Does Marriage Matter?	140
Why Does God Matter?	142
Resources	143
New Books by Barbara Rice	144

Idiot Light

Steve turns a corner driving to work with his carpool buddy. "Oh no!"

"What?" Chad looks up and lays his phone on his knee.

Pointing to the dash, "My Check Marriage light just came on."

"Oh, I hate that. Why don't you just take it in?" Chad looks at Steve.

"My marriage runs fine."

Chad twists his mouth, "Maybe Jeanette knows why it came on. You could ask her."

Steve's mouth drops open, and he pauses. "Well that's like opening a Pandora's box. I'm sure she'd find something wrong. And then after one thing's fixed, it's another. It's never enough. You know? The light keeps coming on."

"Well you shouldn't just ignore it. It's trying to tell you something."

"Used to be in the old days, marriages didn't have all these sensors and crazy lights. You just took her out for dinner every 3,000 miles and you could cruise along for years. Now with all these precise little circuits, you have lights going off every time something's not going right."

Chad sighs. "So whattaya gonna' do about the light?"

"Put some black tape over it."[1]

Reading and discussing the questions in *Tune-Up Your Relationship* can be to your relationship like car maintenance is to your car because problems don't go away on their own. Go ahead. Tune it up! Make your VW run like a Lamborghini!! Enjoy a harmonious and meaningful ride through life to the destination God has planned for you.

CHAPTER ONE: THE ART OF LISTENING

1:1

Bleed Through

"He committed all the sins his father had done before him; his heart was not fully devoted to the Lord his God." I Kings 15:3

A student of mine painted a thick layer of white gesso paint over a brightly painted canvas, but he could still see color. He put layer after layer of white over the canvas, but the colors still bled through, looking like a white-washed flag. We are like that; the attitudes, and actions we experienced growing up can bleed through.

A Dad opens his mouth, and the family hears how Grandpa's anger sounded. A wife distrusts her husband because her father broke her trust. We whitewash our anger: "I don't sound like that!" Or downplay, "I wasn't angry, just irritated." Even with layers of defense and denial, life experiences, like colors, still bleed through, leaving family members feeling unloved, attacked, and unable to trust. Sadly, so many are clueless about their offenses, since the behavior feels normal, having grown up experiencing them, and sometimes we unconsciously react to a prior trauma.

Experiences from our past don't have to overshadow our current lives. After my traumatic childhood, I struggled with neediness, defensiveness, and trust. I found I could give God every hurt I could remember. One by one, I felt each hurt and offered it to God. I listened to what God wanted to give me instead of the hurt. He took each hurt, and I have no more crying little girls in my heart. "Therefore, if anyone is in Christ, the new creation has come: the old has gone, the new is here." 2 Corinthians 5:17

When the pain is from a current relationship, feeling the hurt and then giving it to God helps us start with a clean canvas. Then using "I" statements helps our partners understand how their actions and attitudes affect us without feeding defensiveness. You own the emotion as you share your feelings and experience without accusing your teammate. Sometimes we need a trustworthy counselor, a mentor, or MarriageTeam coach to teach us the skills we need to work through the past to be free, and stop ourselves before we repeat the cycle of allowing prior wounds to bleed through into the lives of our relationships.

Start each day with a clean canvas and paint it with love and truth.

Discussion Questions:

When do you see bleed-through in your spouse? In yourself?

When your spouse is frustrated with you, do you feel safe and loved? Do they feel safe, loved?

Do you feel peaceful about my past?

Prayer:

Lord, bring cleansing and healing to my past wounds.

An "I" statement explains a feeling about an issue without using the word "you". The words "you" enables defensiveness instead of collaboration. An example: "Honey, I feel used and unimportant when I see dirty dishes in the sink not put in the dishwasher. (Remember, an "I" statement doesn't include the word "you.")

1:2

Bearer Or Barrier?

"Carry each other's burdens, and in this way you will fulfill the law of Christ." Galatians 6:2

Grammy held Tyson as Sam walked down the aisle with the flower girl. "Tyson, see Sam? He's the ring bearer."

Tyson stared at Sam, then he put his little hands on Grammy's face and said, "Grammy, if Mommy got married again, could I be her ring barrier?"

Am I a "Bearer" or do I have "Barriers" to love?" Barriers are defenses stemming from old hurts, habits, bitterness, fear, pride, resentments, or judgments. They are the enemy to knowing and being known. Barriers are erected to keep others out.

Before my marriage to Andrew, men I loved let porn or illicit sex rule them. As a result, I found it difficult to believe that my husband would remain faithful to our marriage vows. I put up barriers. How unfair for him to have to earn back trust he'd never broken as the result of the walls I'd built because of my past. "Bearing" my need, he's invited me to check up on him, allowing me to build trust.

Andrew had barriers to love as well. He had developed defense patterns from dysfunctional relationships before he met me.

We have since learned to listen to each other, paraphrasing what the other said and what they felt. Andrew and I often discover our earlier assumptions were wrong. Love's barriers have disappeared. Knowing each other deeply without barriers paves the way to satisfying lifelong love that bears each other's burdens.

Discussion Questions:

What barriers do you bring to your relationship?

What makes it hard for you to listen to your spouse until they feel fully heard and loved?

What changes will you make so your spouse could feel fully heard and understood?

Prayer:

Lord, show me my defenses and the barriers I have built up against love.

1:3

Understanding Understanding

"We put no stumbling block in anyone's path, so that our ministry will not be discredited—in purity, understanding, patience and kindness; in the Holy Spirit and in sincere love in truthful speech—." 2 Corinthians 6:1-7

Winston pursed his lips, "I don't understand. She knew I needed to work late this week."

His wife, Darla, looked away; her lips curved down on one side.

"Hold on." Marriage Coach, Andrew, raised his hand. "It doesn't need to make sense to you. Darla is expressing feelings. Feelings aren't right or wrong; they're feelings." Andrew turned to Darla. "We'd like to hear how you feel about your husband being late for your anniversary dinner. Please turn to Winston and use an 'I' statement about how it felt to have him come home late."

She sighed, "I feel invisible when my needs and desires are ignored or aren't as important as work. I feel like I don't matter."

Winston said, "But you shouldn't feel that way, because I needed to work."

Andrew repeated, "Feelings aren't controlled by 'should.' Darla needs you to understand how she feels whether you agree with her logic. Please repeat back what you heard her say she feels."

Winston did, allowing Darla the opportunity to feel

understood.

Being understanding includes listening to the other person's thoughts and feelings. Judgments kept Winston from understanding because he thought he was right, and that Darla shouldn't feel hurt.

Being understanding doesn't mean you always agree. It means you're wanting to know your partner more, and that you value their feelings.

Since each of us is called by God to be understanding, when we're not, we put a stumbling block in our sweetie's life and discredit the reputation of God by our lack of love. God wants us to show the qualities of 2 Corinthians 6 as a way of loving Him and living out God's mandate of love for the world to see.

Discussion Questions:

When is it hard for you to "be understanding"?

When would you like your spouse to "be understanding"?

How would feeling unheard and not understood affect your relationship with your partner?

Prayer:

Lord, help me seek to understand my spouse with patience and kindness.

1:4

Prickles And Quills And Burrs! Oh My!

"Instead, whoever wants to become great among you must be your servant." Matthew 20:26

Dr. Mark Lauderbach once said people are like porcupines whose quills can hurt if you get too close. Each of us has thousands of "porcupine quills" poking in all directions, the way we do things that may irritate our darling. The only way to live comfortably is to tell each other what hurts, so each partner can adjust and not hurt the other.

This morning as I put on socks, I felt something poking me. When I investigated, I found a tiny round spiny weed seed on the inside of my sock. I couldn't wait to get it out. How much more would your quill bother your partner, digging into them day after day.

After Andrew and I got married, I asked him to keep the toilet lid up, since I used the bathroom at night without turning on the light. He thought it a silly request and made no change, which left me feeling that I didn't matter to him and feeling hurt. Why else would he not consider my needs? When I explained how I felt, he realized the important of this "quill" poke and changed.

I have three choices when poked by my partner's quills: to ask for a change, to endure the pain, or stay apart. We don't have to agree with the reasons the other person gives to explain their hurt to empathize with them. A hurt foot wouldn't need to defend itself to the brain about why it feels pain. The body serves its parts, as we are called to serve each other. It may take many reminders, but freedom from quills is worth the effort to help each other move toward comfort.

Adjusting quills can transform your marriage. Sensitivity to your partner builds trust, and problem-solving conversations form a deeper and deeper sense of feeling known and loved.

Serving the other has two sides, one is sharing with them what you need, so they can love you well, and the other is sensitivity to their hurts and needs, so you can serve them well. Quill pokes drain the happiness from your relationship. Better to adjust and keep the love.

Discussions Questions:

Explain the difference between showing love and just putting up with each other.

How do you and your spouse handle quill pricks?

How would it change your relationship if your spouse made the quill adjustments you need, and you made the adjustments they need?

Prayer:

Lord, help us welcome problem-solving conversations, and seek to be each other's servants.

1:5

The "Know It All"

"Everyone should be quick to listen, slow to speak and slow to become angry, human anger does not bring about the righteous life that God desires." James 1:19-20

I hate talking to a "know-it-all," even more when I realize that the "know-it-all" is me. "Know-it-alls" don't listen to learn. Instead, pride oozes out of us in ways we don't see. It tells people we think we're better than them. It takes humility and love to listen and reflect. Understanding requires being willing to be "wrong" and allowing the other to correct us and clarify. Listening grows humility and love as we realize our assumptions aren't always correct. We listen to know another and help our partner feel known.

Here's an example: Andrew has said, "I hate it when I call your cell phone but can't reach you because the phone isn't with you."

I responded to understand his feelings, "You get frustrated when you can't contact me. Is that right?"

"Yes. Sometimes it's important to ask you a question or give you information. I feel stuck when I need you, and I can't contact you," he said.

"You feel stuck when I'm not available?"

"Yes," Andrew said, feeling heard and understood.

I need to realize that I'm not perfect and adjust accordingly. With humility, I can understand Andrew's feelings and make the changes he needs. When I think I matter more than my partner, I become defensive, and create a battlefield instead of a love nest.

Only God knows everything. The rest of us need to take the time and energy to check with each other to make sure we understand, even when we think we know what the other person is trying to communicate.

Discussions Questions:

How can assuming you know what your partner thinks lead to conflict?

How does it help your relationship to check in with the other to make sure your assumptions are correct?

When do you notice your partner making assumptions that you wish they wouldn't make? How will you handle this in the future?

Prayer:

Lord, give us sensitivity to our honey, and help us make a habit of checking in with them.

1:6

Shame On Me

"I have loved you with an everlasting love; I have drawn you with loving-kindness." Jeremiah 31:3

I developed conjunctivitis because of an extreme allergic reaction which caused my eyes to turn into a putty, sensitive, weepy mess. Every time I saw my reflection, I wanted to cry.

I could see the affection for me in Andrew's eyes as he looked at me during church. I appreciated him loving me, but I wanted to hide.

Shame, a fear of rejection, beckoned me to hide and erect defenses. Like a flash flood, shame washed my logic downstream. Literally, since when we're afraid or angry, our nervous system switches to our sympathetic nervous system, our lower fight-or-flight brain. We cannot access our logic. A blocker to love, self-absorbed and unsympathetic, shame made me blind to the love of God and the love of others. False shame stems from the harsh and often untrue words we hear from others and from ourselves. This shame can define us and warp our perception of who we truly are. The enemy uses shame to accuse us. It exists because we haven't offered our shame to God to comfort, forgive, tell us who we are, and heal us. If we want to flip out the cage of fear and shame, we can offer it to God and thank him that he will bring good out of our worst circumstances. (Romans 8:28) Satan doesn't want me to know that I am God's darling - even with weepy, puffy eyes, but I am.

Discussions Questions:

How do I act when experiencing guilt or shame?

What memory brings me an uncomfortable sense of shame? What prevents me from taking it to God?

How does owning God's forgiveness for myself, help me accept and forgive my partner?

Prayer:

Lord, I give you my wrongdoings or belief that I'm not enough. You already paid for my atonement. I give you my shame for what I have done and what I have not done. I receive your forgiveness, asking for the Holy Spirit's control in my life as I surrender to the God who loves me.

1:7

Color Blind

"For anyone who does not love his brother and sister, whom he has seen, cannot love God." 1 John 4:20

Our son is color blind, and we bought him color-correcting glasses. He put them on for the first time and cried. He looked at the Christmas wrapping paper and said, "That's teal, isn't it? People have been talking about teal all my life, and I never knew what they were taking about."

Sometimes our marriages are like that. We don't realize that our vision isn't perfect. It's all we've ever known. We all have blind spots in our lives, areas where we can't spot the pattern or differentiate healthy behaviors from unhealthy ones. The only way to change is by being willing to face the fact that we have an imperfect vision. Being willing to use "I" statements, speaking and listening with the goal of love, is like putting on color-correcting glasses. We see details and colors we might have missed before because our former way of talking and listening (or not listening) created defensiveness and conflict, impeding our ability to perceive our honey accurately.

Put on love glasses by asking God to help you see the way He sees and communicate in the colors and ways your beloved needs to feel loved.

(To some, receiving a hug or physical touch means love, to another, hearing affirming words means the most, others, time together talking, getting presents, or having something done for them, like a chore or task. For more information, see Gary Chapman's book, The Five Love Languages: The Secret to Love That Lasts.)

Discussion Questions:

Tell each other which of the five are your favorite ways of receiving love.

What are the benefits of telling each other our preferences and showing appreciation for the love that's shown?

How does presuming you know everything there is about your spouse keep you from discovering more about them and loving them better?

Prayer:

Lord, help me always keep learning how to love.

CHAPTER TWO: THE ART OF SPEAKING

2:1

Bombing

"Do not let any unwholesome words come out of your mouths, but only what is helpful for building others up according to their needs, that it may benefit those who listen." Ephesians 4:29

Shaking, Nan Abbott heard the siren and grabbed her toddler from his bed and the baby from her crib and ran with her children in her arms to the bomb shelter, still in her pajamas. Planes fingered their way through the London fog in the early morning. German pilots dived, dropped bombs, killed close to 30,000 people, decimating the city, never to be forgotten.

We don't mean to declare war on our spouses. We don't start out wanting to bomb their self-esteems with our words echoing forever in their memories. What we want is our way. If someone, even our teammate, gets in our way, we might open the hatch and let the bombs fall. We blame it on a stressful day, being tired, or feeling upset.

But we don't have to fly loaded, as if we're going to war. Jesus said, "Come to me, all you who are weary and burdened, and I will give you rest." Matthew 11:28 NIV. He is waiting for us to come to Him with our stress. There are no excuses for bombing someone with hurtful words.

There are many kinds of bombs: playing a martyr to get the upper-hand, over-talking, attacking the other's character, changing the subject so we never "lose" an argument, bringing up past errors, silence, or refusing to negotiate. These have the power to destroy love. They may win the battle but will lose the war. Our mouths, like the opening in planes that drop bombs, can be controlled. We are called to only say what is helpful for others, building them, benefiting them according to Ephesians 4:29.

Shower instead with powerful words of affirmation. Appreciation like complaining can become a habit. The habit of giving positive words rains down joy and love to the giver and the receiver.

Discussion Questions:

What triggers you to unleash a bomb of harsh words? Why?

How can you learn to hear the way you sound to others?

What is the long-term effect of letting angry emotions fly?

Prayer:

Lord, teach me to love.

2:2

Fib Or Fact

"Therefore, rejecting all falsehood, (whether lying, defrauding, telling half-truths, spreading rumors, any such as these), speak truth each one with his neighbor, for we are all parts of one another (and we are all parts of the body of Christ." Ephesians 4:25 Amplified

Five-year-old Kaden came running as I pulled out his gift - a Batman blanket, "I'm fibbergasted!" he replied, bouncing. He "fibbed" about being "flabbergasted".

I laughed since I too get "fibbergasted." I sometimes fib; when asked a question, answering with what *feels* right rather than what *is* right. Then I consider my answer, and I'm flabbergasted because I wasn't accurate. None of us tell the truth *all* the time. We mean to, but sometimes we don't quite get it right, or we leave a part out. Sometimes, we don't want to appear incompetent, stupid or unloving, so we exaggerate or lie. We care more about what others think than telling the truth.

It never pays to break God's principles. God will make sure my lying won't benefit me. If I'm trying to be impressive, others will see my pretense. If I'm trying to gain an advantage by lying, I'm apt to be caught and pay a bigger price. Most of all, those I depend on to love me will see that I'm lying and lose respect for me. Kids remember the worst in us and use it to justify the worst of choices for themselves.

I can catch myself at the moment and pray for God's Spirit to speak truth through me, leaving the results with him. Living in God's victory and love is the most powerful tool to keep from being "fibbergasted." When I'm abiding in him, I'm not apt to lie to gain the approval of people.

In a romantic relationship, the basis for our trust depends on the other's reliable words and actions. If our partner habitually lies or acts unloving, we have no basis for trust in any arena. It's essential to let your partner know in a non-threatening way when you feel lied to. Lies, in all their forms, wash acid onto trust, dissolving the glue that keeps us together—trust. Tell the truth to live in harmony.

Discussion Questions:

When is it hard for me to tell the truth?

What do I gain by lying?

How can I pray when tempted to lie?

Prayer:

Lord, help me tell the truth.

2:3

Love That Tone!

"The tongue that brings healing is a tree of life, but a deceitful tongue crushes the spirit." Proverbs 15:4

Katie pressed into the tabletop with shaking hands. "Bert, I can't hear your words, anger is all I can hear. I feel hurt and threatened when someone throws angry words at me. I'll make dinner now. Let's talk about this another time when we can talk without anger."

Bert stared at her for a moment before stomping off. He wanted to MAKE her listen. He knew he was right. But why did she feel hurt? He needed to think about it.

Communications experts tell us that the biggest part of communication is nonverbal. More information gets communicated by the tone of our voice than the meanings of our words. Couples can mock with the inflections in their voices. Body language can say, "I'm better than you." Contempt can speak through even a quiet tone. Sheer volume can intimidate. Bullying comes in many forms. When criticism, contempt, and anger vent, we destroy the people in the path.

By processing my feelings with God before I throw them at those I love, I can allow God, the one who loves me beyond my imagination, to take my fears, filter out the truth from emotion. Then I'm more prepared to speak the truth with a tone of voice that can be heard without barriers.

My daughter, Brenna, does it this way—she's figured out

that the first voice she hears in her own head is her own drama, so she ignores the first voice and waits for the second voice, the voice of reason.

People forget what we say, but not how they felt after we said it.

Discussion Questions:

How does an angry voice affect you?

How can you communicate kindly when feeling frustrated or angry?

What change can help you and your spouse communicate with kindness when angry?

Prayer:

Lord, help me speak the truth in love. If I have experienced anger growing up, help me dig out the hurt I've received and give it to you before it owns me and my family.

2:4

Loving Correction

"Better is an open reprimand (of loving correction) Than love that is hidden. Faithful are the wounds of a friend (who corrects out of love and concern), But the kisses of an enemy are deceitful (because they serve his hidden agenda). Proverbs 27:5-6 Amplified

We need equal relationships so that neither of us is intimidated to tell the other the truth they need, in a loving way. This passage implies that giving each other loving correction is part of being a friend. People who flatter me to get what they want from me are not my friends.

People can create relationships with someone who fits them in dysfunctional ways, not having equality in their relationship. I grew up with a father who didn't allow me to own myself. It took me decades to grow into the ability to have equal relationships. I hid my feelings, afraid if I spoke the truth to my boyfriend or husband, I wouldn't be safe just like when I grew up. I fit with someone who would take responsibility for me. It's felt uncomfortable at times, but I've learned that speaking truth to my spouse is part of friendship and part of love.

Under-talking and over-talking can get in the way of equal relationships. Over-talking wears out listeners and prevents the under-talker from expressing themselves as fully. Under-talkers keep themselves from feeling known by not revealing much about themselves.

If over-talking or under-talking has become a habit, you might try growing your relationship to a deeper level. Going on "Walk-Talks" may help. One person talks for a set amount of time, and then the other takes a turn.

Constantly wounding our spouses with truth that we think they need, or over-talking as we correct our beloved, can make a relationship too painful to bear, though we all need loving correction at times. By not over or under talking, we can gently make our point and move on.

The One-Minute Manager by Kenneth H. Blanchard helped me learn to say what I wanted in one minute, helping me think about what I wanted to say before I share. Now, my husband and I can both enjoy sharing our dreams, feelings, plans, and occasionally gently correct each other.

Discussion Questions:

How would you want your honey to approach giving you advice or correction?

How can the correction of someone who knows you well help you?

Why would a couple want both parties to talk for the same amount of time? Why not?

Prayer:

Lord, whatever my natural temperament, give me the vision and ability to discover and help my spouse.

2:5

Mercy Wins!

"Speak and act as those who are going to be judged by the law that gives freedom, because judgment without mercy will be shown to anyone who has not been merciful. Mercy triumphs over judgment!" James 2:12

Diane was in the kitchen making sandwiches for the family when she heard screams. When she reached the apartment's pool, she saw her sister-in-law frantically trying to locate Diane's three-year-old son, Vincent, who had been riding his trike near the water with his cousins. A relative pulled out an inflatable mattress floating in the pool and found the toddler. Not breathing.

I asked Diane how she and her husband stayed close in their marriage while over half of couples who lose a child in a tragic accident end up filing for divorce. She said they stayed in love, not anger, and refused to let "what if" thoughts attack their minds. They stayed close to their support group at church as they realized that Vincent's death devastated the entire community, not only their family. They dove into the book of Job and waited on God. Diane expected God to comfort others through His comfort to them. Later, she led grief classes and noticed something astounding: couples who felt intense anger when they began the grief group stayed stuck in anger throughout the time. Couples who started with love and forgiveness stayed in love. Diane and her husband allowed more of God's grace into their hearts and marriage, which kept revenge and anger from owning them. As a result, they have been peaceful even though grieving.

The more wounded we feel, the more of God's love and grace we need. If we speak from a core of anger, our words of judgment not only destroy those who hear but prevent us from the mercy we need to be healed.

Discussion Questions:

What does it mean to speak to our spouse with mercy?

How does speaking with mercy sound and feel different from speaking with judgment?

What needs to change for us to speak with mercy?

Prayer:

Lord, keep us daily living in your mercy.

2:6

Wise Investors

"Whatever is true, whatever is noble, whatever is right, whatever is pure, whatever is lovely, whatever is admirable—if anything is excellent or praiseworthy —think about such things." Philippians. 4:8

My mother's cousin, Lois, is 97 and doesn't drive, so I sometimes took her to her appointments. One day I asked her how she was feeling, and she replied, "Don't ask me that; I'm an old woman."

Lois knows dwelling on her aches and pains, or focusing on what is negative in her life, brings everyone down. It's a mindset choice for her. Lois wants to focus on what's good, so she filled her marriage with constant supportive conversations. She and her husband discussed their frustrations, resolving them, but Lois pointed her husband and children to love by focusing herself on love and encouragement.

Dr. John Gottman wrote about what made happy marriages and why they broke down in his book *Why Marriage Succeed or Fail*.

"We have found that it all comes down to a simple mathematical formula: no matter what style your marriage follows, you must have at least five times as many positive as negative moments together if your marriage is to be stable."[2]

The author of love, God, mandates that we focus of what

is beautiful and excellent in Philippians 4:8. It's counterculture for us. We may need to resist our culture to be positive. Those around us may complain as a lifestyle, but their lives will not display the joy and purpose God desires for his children.

Noticing what is worthy of praise in the world around us and especially in my spouse, enriches my marriage, feeds the heart of my beloved, and sets an example for our children and the world to see and follow.

Discussion Questions:

What do you appreciate about your spouse?

How does it feel when your spouse is critical of you?

How can you change your attitude when you feel like being critical?

Prayer:

Lord, help me focus on what is beautiful in my spouse.

2:7

Different, Not Dominant

"If it is possible, as far it depends on you, live at peace with everyone." Romans 12:18

Baby Lilli snuggled in Grammy's arms all morning, not her usual lively self. She ate little for lunch and then had diarrhea. Twenty-four hours later, Papa and Grammy's stomachs churned, ached, and soon emptied. Both grandparents experienced the same symptoms but attributed them to different diagnoses. Papa had been sick from food poisoning before, and this felt the same. He went to work. Grammy believed they had the flu. Lilli exposed them. Simple. Both flu and food poisoning have the same symptoms.

This could create a battle of wills. He might have yelled at her for not throwing away the spinach, which he thought caused the food poisoning. She could have gotten upset with him for not staying home, but they realized that their perspectives were different and gave the other person grace to think differently. One is not responsible for the other's actions nor opinions.

In important decisions, prayer, sharing perspectives, investigating options, problem-solving and getting wise counsel could help a couple make a unified decision. With minor issues, freedom to choose independently allows a couple breathing room.

Discussion Questions:

Do couples need the same opinions? Why? Why not?

If one partner demands agreement from the other, how would it impact their relationship?

In what areas do you need agreement and in what areas do you want the freedom to disagree?

Prayer:

Lord, thank you, you give us freedom to choose, fail or succeed and learn. Help us allow our partners to do the same.

CHAPTER THREE: ANNOYING ANGER

3:1

Rubbing Up Against Shame

"Adam and his wife were both naked, and they felt no shame." Genesis 2:25

The Garden of Eden burst with beauty and freedom. Adam and Eve studied the animals together and decided on the names that best fit the animals. They walked with God every day and lived in harmony. But once rebellion entered their hearts, Eve and then Adam ate the only fruit they weren't allowed to eat. They flunked the test and kicked God out of their lives. *I'll do it my way, God. I don't want you.* A new era began. The first demon to reveal its head was shame resulting in blame. Adam blamed Eve. Eve blamed the serpent. Their child, Cain, murdered his brother, shamed that Abel's gift was accepted by God and his not.

Since anger is a secondary emotion. Cain first felt shame and then anger that his gift wasn't accepted. If he would have told God, "I feel ashamed that you didn't accept my gift. Show me how to please you so my gifts will be accepted," his anger would have quelled. Once we don't speak the truth in love, (Ephesians 4:15) our brain flips to its reactionary side, and we act or talk out sometimes before we think through what we're doing or saying.

The trick is to catch yourself at the hurt stage and express the hurt appropriately. Sheldon said, "Honey, I feel frustrated when someone leaves my car seats littered with junk. I feel my preferences to keep my car tidy don't matter." By using the "I" statement and speaking the truth lovingly, Sheldon short-circuited the body's usual path to act out anger without thinking. He obeyed Ephesians 4:15 and spoke the truth about how he felt in a loving manner.

Discussion Questions:

What is the hurt that often triggers your anger?

How could you react differently if you caught the hurt before it expressed itself as anger?

How can your spouse help you with the vulnerable places in you?

Prayer:

Lord, help me recognize the hurts I feel and express them appropriately.

3:2

The Same Shame/Blame

"Discretion will protect you, and understanding will guard you." Proverbs 2:11

When in a relationship, we're bound to expose our partner's faults at some point or another. Even if it's inadvertently, we will do something that triggers their shame by revealing something they don't know or exposes their inability to do something. When that happens, guilt and shame often trigger hostility toward the person they deem responsible for making them feel ashamed.

Here's an example of shame. Paul snapped at Janis when he had to wait for her to get ready for church. Paul felt angry about her making him late. Why? Because when he was late, he felt like a failure. Why? Because he felt if he didn't show that he was responsible for being on time, Dad wouldn't accept him. Why did that matter? Because he felt he needed Dad's approval to be a man. Being late was shameful.

Tracing anger back to the lie triggering the emotion helps us resolve those feelings in a healthy manner. When Paul realized his anger presented itself when someone made him late, he could ask himself the "why" questions and realize he didn't need Dad's approval; he needed God's. Once he could acknowledge that, being late wouldn't hold shame for him anymore. We can clean our hearts of trigger points by paying attention to what brings us shame or anger. When our beloved's reaction or our reaction seems bigger than the offense, it's probably due to a hurt and lie based on something from the past.

Janis can try to not make Paul late, but if she realizes Paul's hostility stems from his misdirected sense of shame and a lie he believes, it might be easier for her not to take his reaction personally and escalate the tension in the home by responding to his hurt with her own.

When we feel our emotions balloon, we can think through why we feel the way we do and pray for the truth in the situation to be revealed. Understanding ourselves and God's wisdom can set us free!

Discussion Questions:

Can telling the person who hurt you *that* you are hurt help free you of anger?

Have the fires of anger hurt you or anyone close to you?

What is behind the anger stored in your heart?

Prayer:

Lord, help me recognize the process of hurt unrevealed turning to anger, so I can more quickly give my hurts to you.

3:3

Passing Off My Past

"Who will bring any charge against those whom God has chosen? It is God who justifies." Romans 8:33

As a child I learned that not all people are kind. In the world, we're surrounded by criticism, comparison, and verbal attacks. We're only human. I forget, make mistakes, get confused, don't know everything I need to know, and make bad choices. But no one has the right to bring any charge against me, only Christ, who died to pay for all my failings. What a life changer for me to realize that God has forgiven all wrong I have ever done and could ever do, and only God has the right to judge my life. When I surrendered my life to him, He took all that would bring me shame, and obliterated it.

Then, why do I still feel ashamed when I fall short? Because I agree with the demons that say I'm not free of condemnation instead of believing the words of Christ who died to free me. When I focus on the way I think others see me, I'm behaving as if I care more about what others think of me than I care about how God sees me.

When I accept the lies and twisted words of the enemy, I don't take the seeds of truth and plant them in my heart, making them my own. I don't weed out the lies and throw them away. And then I wonder why I bear little of the fruit of the Spirit: love, joy, peace, patience, kindness, goodness, faithfulness, gentleness, and self-control. (Galatians 5:22—

23)
In relationships, we can help each other live in freedom by not judging each other or ourselves. DeAnn, as an example, hears her husband under his breath say, "Toast from hell," about her burnt toast. She speaks to him using gentle and encouraging words. "Honey, I'm sorry the toast is black on the edges. Do you want a fresh piece? I know you do appreciate me fixing you breakfast." Living forgiven and living out forgiveness with each other allows the Holy Spirit to breathe through us as individuals and through our relationship.

Discussions Questions:

How does Christ's payment for all the wrongs you've done affect how you live?

If you are forgiven of all your wrongdoings, how does it affect you when your teammate offends you?

If only Christ has the right to judge, how does that affect how you talk to yourself and to others?

Prayer:

Lord, I give you my right to criticize others and myself.

3:4

Using Anger For Good

"In your anger, do not sin: Do not let the sun go down while you are still angry." Ephesians. 4:26

Jane pleaded with her husband to show her compassion. She used word pictures, conversations timed after food and rest, books she'd picked up on marriage, and counseling, but he refused to change. After sixteen years of trying to help him understand her needs, sixteen years of telling herself not to slam her car into the concrete abutment next to the road she traveled every day because she felt so alone and depressed, enduring a relationship devoid of affection and love, she told him she was divorcing him. She had no energy nor hope left for the relationship. His mouth dropped open. He didn't understand what had happened. He'd discounted her pain for decades, and eventually, her hope disappeared.

Her anger affected her health. Their children, too, carried their mother's hurt and anger, not understanding that it was not their fault. She felt depressed and overate to compensate.

Since we're human, we will feel hurt and then anger, but the family's wellbeing depends on conflict and resulting anger being resolved, and not stored.

A rattle in the engine would signal that something in the motor needs addressing. Listening to each other is like listening to the sound of your motor, it tells you if your relationship is humming or not.

An "I" statement can help. Jane said to her husband, "I feel hopeless when I'm expressing my feelings, and it seems like the cell phone takes precedent over my conversation. I feel unknown and lonely." But the listener needs to take seriously the needs of his spouse as well.

Anger, like a high fever, warrants quick evaluation. Otherwise, we alter our memories and alienate those we love. With time, our minds distort information. Anger, given an opportunity to fester, eats at our hearts, taxes our bodies, and destroys our relationships. Express you hurt quickly.

Discussion Questions:

Do you have stuffed concerns that warrant discussion?

How can you process anger, so it doesn't destroy you?

How can "I feel" statements help with anger?

Prayer:

Lord, give me wisdom and to tell a person in a kind way that they hurt me.

3:5

Climbing The Wrong Tree!

"Human anger does not product the righteousness that God desires about the righteous life that God desires... Those who consider themselves religious and yet do not keep a tight rein on their tongues deceive themselves, and their religion is worthless." James 1: 20 & 26

Monte saw how much food his wife, Nancy, brought home. He was furious. He had told her not to buy so much, but she's insisted on stocking up at sales. Then she wore that hurt, helpless look on her face. He hated that she looked as if he'd slapped her.

They'd had this fight before, and Nancy knew how he felt about her overspending, which justified the anger coming through the tone of his voice, he thought. But his words were eroding their marriage. Nancy had done her best to save money by shopping the sales, but she also wanted to make sure that her family had enough food in the cupboards. They both were convinced that they were right, and that the other was being unreasonable and unsupportive. Thus, another familiar round of spats began. Each tried to prove their points, climbing a metaphorical ladder which stood against the tree of "Being Right". Each tried to climb higher than the other to justify their position.

Once they realized they were climbing the wrong tree and moved on to focusing on love: understanding and being understood, their methods and purposes changed. When Monte expressed his fear about not having enough money using an "I" statement saying how he felt like a failure when they didn't have a margin of extra money, Nancy could understand without feeling hurt. Nancy used an "I" statement to tell Monte how hearing critical and angry words made her feel worthless and unconnected, and he changed the way he spoke. As he sought to understand her reasons behind buying sales, they decided on a set amount of money for sale items that they would need in the future.

It's easy to climb the ladder against the "Being Right" tree. Moving the ladder to the "Love" tree works better. It's the only one with sweet fruit.

Discussions Questions:

What effect would it have if you used "I" statements instead of expressing anger when you're frustrated?

How could you ask your sweetheart to pray for you?

What will it cost your family if you don't change how you and your spouse communicate with each other?

Prayer:

Lord, make me aware when I'm seeking to be right instead of understanding my beloved.

3:6

Patience

"A hot-tempered man stirs up dissension, but a patient man calms a quarrel." Proverbs 15:18

Brandon's eyes flamed as he screamed at me. My natural tendency is to run from anger, but Proverb 15:18 says it's possible at times, with patience, to calm a quarrel. This time, instead of bolting, I sought to find out what was going on underneath the surface of the wrath that was being targeted at me. I repeated his statements, so he knew I was listening, and could feel understood. Then I asked him what he needed. I praised him for anything he'd done worthy of praise. Everything changed. He couldn't excuse his own behavior, because I hadn't taken the bait and started screaming back at him. Instead, he realized at least some blame about the situation rested on him. We could problem-solve when we both felt understood.

If a person is yelling, it is appropriate to ask them to talk later when they can be calm. Words spoken in anger are seldom true and are a weapon. Receiving the anger or angry words at face value won't calm the quarrel. With patience, it's possible to find out what's under the anger—the hurt and or fear the angry person is feeling at the moment. Understanding first, then problem-solving.

But not every heated conversation goes that way.

When someone is physically, emotionally, or verbally abusive, they need professional help. Too many people stay in an abusive environment, not realizing that abuse tends to get worse over time.

Whether you address someone's anger immediately, or later, when they're able to express their feelings with an even tone of voice, we all need patience to help each other feel understood. We can either live a life full of dissension because of our temper, or a calm life because of our patience. The choice is ours.

Discussion Questions:

How patience in conflict help, and how does anger in conflict hurt the relationship?

What do you need from your spouse when you're angry?

Would you like God to help you? Can you ask Him?

Prayer:

Lord, give me wisdom, discernment and patience when dealing with an angry person.

3:7

Fabric Fury

"A gentle answer turns away wrath, but a harsh word stirs up anger." Proverbs 15:1

We only had twenty minutes before we needed to go to our MarriageTeam coaches' meeting. It was just enough time to stop and pick up some fabric I'd been wanting. I promised I'd be back in time and left Andrew waiting in the car. I gave myself ten minutes to look, but then the clerk wasn't available to cut my fabric. Then when she came, she took her time. I went to pay, but several others were in front of me. Andrew called on my cell phone angry. The clerk, hearing it, became flustered and messed up the cash register tally. She had to ring the purchase again. Andrew called again, assuming I could just put my cut fabric back on a shelf and walk out of the store without paying. To him, I'd broken my promise. Because neither of us spoke the truth gently, we both felt hurt, misunderstood, and angry.

I'd love to say we talked through it immediately using "I" statements about how we felt, we're marriage coaches, but we rushed off to our meeting feeling ripped apart inside. Only later did we gently express our feelings without blame. Once we both understood, the rift between us disappeared.

We don't necessarily use "I" statements in conversations where there's little threat of someone feeling hurt or attacked, but when either of you has a lot of emotion about the subject at hand, using an "I" statement can allow sharing without defensiveness. Ironically, when we feel a lot of emotion about something, we tend to flip into our fight-or-flight brain and have no access to the logic part of our brains. The longer we stew on our hurt, the more bitterness and distortion take over leading to contempt. It's essential to recognize what's happening in your relationship. Once we observe that we or the other person is hurt or angry, then it's time to flip into using "I" statements. "I felt hurt when—" can bring healing even when it seems impossible.

Discussion Questions:

Why is it so important not to make assumptions?

How do assumptions fight against trust?

How can using an "I" statement help a conversation not feel like an attack?

Prayer:

Lord, help me listen to understand a situation from my spouse's perspective before I speak or react to it.

CHAPTER FOUR: GIVING FORGIVENESS

4:1

Love your Enemy

"Love your enemies and pray for those who persecute you." Matthew 5:44

I stood overlooking the Willamette River pleading with God to help me not hate my boss. I was trapped in a job I couldn't quit, working for a boss I hated. After hearing his lies spread throughout the business and being the target of his contempt, I writhed with anger.

"God, I don't want to hate him, but I do. Help me," I said.

The reply rang in my heart, "That's because you haven't loved your enemy."

I was shocked that I heard God so clearly, but even more by what He said! "What? Love Brett?" I calmed myself. "Okay, God, I'll gossip less." I compromised.

A month went by, and I returned to the river to pray. I still felt helpless, angry, and tortured. "God, I still hate him." I confessed.

Again, God said, "Love your enemy."

I shook my head. "Okay, but I need you do this through me. I can't."

Within the week, the Holy Spirit led me to buy a greeting card that I knew Brett would like, and later to send flowers for his dinner party. A slow-motion miracle happened over time as I continued to give. I didn't feel "under" him anymore. I felt in control of myself. Then it hit me. Loving my enemy is primarily for *me*. Even though Brett didn't change, showing love to him freed me to find the peace that I was lacking.

Discussion Questions:

Can you let God be in control of dealing with your enemy?

How can we forgive when we feel like the other person doesn't deserve it?

How does it change us when we forgive others?

Prayer:

Lord, I give you the one who hurt me. Show me how to give love to them.

4:2

Forgiveness Doesn't Mean Trust

"Father, forgive them, for they do not know what they are doing." Luke 23:34

Leilani rose to use the bathroom in the night and noticed her husband, Ron, wasn't in bed. She found him watching porn in his office on his computer. He blamed it on pop-ups, but when she looked at the computer's history, daily porn usage was clear.

Ron asked her to forgive him, sagging like a willow tree. When she said, "I forgive you, but you broke my trust," he looked shocked.

In a coaching session, Leilani said to him, "Your marriage vows are a lie. How can I trust you?"

Ron sat up, "You said you forgave me."

Andrew, the marriage coach, said, "Forgiveness isn't the same as trust. Jesus called us to forgive, to release the wrongness of the offense for God to judge. But trust requires a wise risk. Ron, you broke your marriage vows both to be faithful and love her. And, when you don't love your spouse, you offend God as well. You needed to confess your unfaithfulness to God and to Leilani."

Ron needed to earn back trustworthiness through accountability. Those addicted to porn need to spend a year or more in a Celebrate Recovery group or agreeing to taking part in counseling and having someone check his computer history and behavior to verify change before their beloved would be wise to trust them. The longer Ron had been using porn, the more intense his treatment would need to be. Leilani's "I" statement about how his pornography use made her feel, could help him to gain empathy, but Pornography use is extremely addictive.

Leilani could begin the process of forgiveness immediately, for her sake and Ron's. She could express to Ron her hurt. He could ask her to forgive him. Even if he didn't ask for forgiveness, or if he continued to re-offend, she could forgive. Otherwise, she wouldn't have peace. But, even in aligning with him in his struggle, she can help him most by holding him accountable, not trusting him before he's proven his trustworthiness.

Celebrate Recovery offers groups for spouses of sex addicts and groups for addicts to give support and perspective. Pornography changes attitudes about a woman's value. Addiction destroys intimacy thus intimacy requires support and trust to rebuild.

Discussion Questions:

How does trust develop?

Why is trust important?

Once you've broken trust, what could you do to restore it?

Prayer:

Lord, give me the courage to show tough love when another person needs accountability. Bring me your perspective and the strength to be faithful and trustworthy.

4:3

Speaking The Truth Frees *You*

"Speaking the truth in love, we will in all things grow up into him who is the Head, that is Christ." Ephesians 4:15

Brita's face hardened for a moment as she thought about her husband, Tony, leaving the house to go hunting for two weeks. Pangs of loneliness and a sense of abandonment taunted her when she was left alone. *I know I shouldn't feel this way*, she thought when Tony left. When he returned, she'd act out her hurt by ignoring him and getting snappy. Then she'd think about how selfish she'd been for wanting him to give up hunting to appease her and feel guilty for desiring that he foregoes his favorite sport, but the resentment wouldn't go away.

Some of us grow up under the adage, "Children are to be seen and not heard." If we grow up with needs, strong feelings, or wants that are dismissed as unimportant, we can grow into adults uncomfortable with vocalizing our desires and needs because we wrongly believe that our feelings don't matter. Jesus welcomes us to tell him our needs in Matthew 11:28, "Come to me, all you who are weary and burdened, and I will give you rest."

Jesus not only wants us to tell him our wants and needs, he wants us to tell each other the truth about ourselves. Instead of scheming and manipulating others to get what we want, we are to speak the truth in love. (Ephesians 4:15). Speaking the truth is the road to forgiveness and harmony.

With the support of her MarriageTeam Coaches, Brita told Tony, "I feel lonely and abandoned when I'm left alone because it feels like no one wants me." She stopped storing up hurts by expressing them. Then Tony and Brita problem solved, satisfying his desire to get away and her desire to feel connected, not abandoned.

Brita grew in honesty rather than collecting offenses she hadn't forgiven, and Tony learned to how to help Brita feel loved and connected.

Discussion Questions:

Would you want to know if any of your behaviors irritate your spouse?

Are there irritations you'd like to discuss?

What keeps you from speaking the truth about your frustrations lovingly?

Prayer:

Lord, help me speak the truth in love, making sure I express my concerns in a gentle but honest way.

4:4

To Forgive Or Not To Forgive

"And when you stand praying, if you hold anything against anyone, forgive him, so that your Father in Heaven may forgive you your sins." Mark 11:25

Janis lived a silent scream. A drunk driver had killed her only child. Every morning, pain slapped her anew. How could she forgive the killer? Life had lost all color. She couldn't face entering her daughter's bedroom to clean it, so a year went by with the girl's door never opening. Since people can't shut down part of their emotions without damping down all of them, loving her husband, friends, and God became a chore. Her daily energy emptied by maintaining her quiet rage. Healing eluded her until she forgave the man who drove the car. When she kept judgement as her right, God couldn't take the pain from her. The day she gave God her hurt, she saw a vision of her daughter's smiling face. She was with God. An enormous weight lifted off Janis. God may not give everyone visions, but he longs to bring peace and healing. As Psalm 30:2 says, "Lord, my God, I called to you for help, and you healed me." NIV

Janis and her husband turned around their failing marriage. Instead of being stuck in her sorrow, she and her husband could love each other.

Discussion Questions:

Is there someone you don't want to go to heaven?

How would it free you to leave "justice" with God?

Will you leave justice to God and not try bringing about justice yourself?

Prayer:

Lord, I choose forgiveness, help me go through my memories and give those who hurt me to you, forgiving those who hurt me and forgiving myself. Heal me, Lord.

4:5

Expectations 101

"Clothe yourselves with compassion, kindness, humility, gentleness and patience. Bear with each other and forgive whatever grievances you may have against one another." Colossians 3:12–13

Shanna's dad kept up the yard, the cars, home repairs, and even created woodcarvings on the side. After she married Noble, she assumed she didn't have to get her car's oil changed, Noble should do it. He never did. Oops, her car had major motor trouble. They couldn't afford to buy another car. Noble couldn't believe Shanna could be so irresponsible. She felt betrayed that Noble hadn't looked after her car.

In today's cultures, more than ever, expectations without agreements are like filling a gas tank with water and thinking the car will run because you want it to.

Just as birds build a nest from scratch, finding one twig and then another to weave together to build a home for themselves and their babies, so a couple both brings parts of themselves to weave in with the other, bending and making allowances for the other where needed. People are complex, yet two different people with different needs can talk through their needs and make a tight, sweet nest. By working together and forgiving the mistakes and imperfections in each other, our relationships can become sweeter as time goes by.

Discussion Questions:

What do you expect of your mate? (Physically, mentally, spiritually, socially, financially, at home, with kids, with in-laws etc.)

Why?

Do you both agree to these expectations?

Prayer:

Lord, help us understand what we're expecting of our teammate and what they're expecting of us.

4:6

Forgiveness Versus Retaliation

"Be kind and compassionate to one another, forgiving each other, just as in Christ God forgave you." Ephesians 4:32

When Brittany sent birthday invitations through the mail to people at church, Carl, her husband, said, "What did you do that for? You could have handed them out. Sometimes, you don't use your head." Brittany went in the garage and screamed. She couldn't do anything right. Well, maybe she'd sleep in the extra bedroom for a while, a long while.

Carl wasn't trying to be cruel. He thought handing the invitations out at church would save money. Brittany thought that receiving a postal delivery would feel more special. Because they didn't agree and neither was willing to communicate their thoughts and feelings, another rift began.

Brittany created a separation to "show him" instead of speaking the truth using "I" statements. The kids picked up on mom's hurt. Their son became distant, and their daughter decided she wouldn't ever get married.

(We are not suggesting someone stay in an abusive relationship. If a man is hitting his wife, she needs to get out. Studies show that abuse gets worse, not better over time. The man who abuses his wife needs serious, long-term help. She is being a crutch instead of helping him face his issues by staying. Additional harm is likely to come to her and her children if she's too afraid to leave or denies that there's a problem. With all forms of abuse, she needs help.)

But when marital problems revolve around irritation about one partner doing or not doing something that displeases us, the choice to forgive rather than retaliate makes all the difference between living in a love nest or in a caged cat fight.

Discussion Questions:

What do you do when feeling angry and want to get even?

What could you do that would have a positive outcome?

How does retaliation keep a relationship in turmoil?

Prayer:

Lord, help me show care without defensiveness or vengeance.

4:7

Poor Me!

"For if you forgive men when they sin against you, your heavenly Father will also forgive you. But if you do not forgive me their sins, your Father will not forgive your sins." Matthew 6:14-15

Samantha frowned as she spoke of her hurt. "He ruined my life," speaking of her former husband. The tone of her voice told me that the memories owned her. "He left me." She didn't want to forgive him, which kept her a slave to self-pity, locked to the worst moments of her life. Perhaps her hardness and lack of forgiveness also kept him from wanting to reconcile with her. Now she struggles with obesity, depression, and diabetes, which she blamed on her previous husband. I wanted to cry when I last visited her. Her energy focused on defending herself, since she viewed herself as a victim. If all those wonderful traits she possessed were channeled to love and fulfill God's purpose for her, she could be living a completely different life.

Oswald Chambers said in *My Utmost for His Highest,* "No sin is worse than the sin of self-pity because it removes God from the throne of our lives, replacing Him with our own self-interests. It causes us to open our mouths only to complain, and we become spiritual sponges—always absorbing, never giving, and never being satisfied. And there is nothing lovely or generous about our lives." (May 16).

Human nature wants to focus on our own hurts. Like

picking at a scab, instead of leaving it alone, the wound can't heal and remains the focus of our lives. Thinking about the wrongs we've sustained becomes a habit, so we don't notice our thoughts have become self-focused, imagining scenes to suit our ego's desires. Saying, "Thank you, God, that You can take every part of my life and use it for good. I forgive the person who hurt me," brings me healing, especially when I don't want to pray that prayer. It can begin the process of freedom. Changing habits from victimhood to victory may take time but casting out lies about my plight and focusing on the gifts I have, is the path to peace.

Discussion Questions:

What offenses keep creeping into your memories?

If your spouse sees that you're holding onto unforgiveness, do you want them to tell you?

How can telling God "thank you for using even evil actions for good," set you free?

Prayer:

Lord, I offer to you the one who hurt me. As I give them to you, what do you want to put into my hands in place of my anger and hurt? (Listen to God to see what he wants to give you in place of your hurt and anger.)

CHAPTER FIVE: RESOLVING CONFLICT

5:1

Entitlement: The Right That's Wrong

"God opposes the proud but gives grace to the humble." James 4:6

John never seemed to get the love he was looking for from his wife and family. Because he wasn't receiving what he expected, he became demanding of those around him. The more he demanded love, the more his friends and family pulled away, and the more dissatisfied he became. His wife and children felt like they were never good enough for him, because he focused on his desires rather than their need for affirmation and acceptance.

Curious, I asked him, "Are you smarter and more important than the rest of your family?"

He answered with a sly smile. "I *am* the man of the family."

When love is seen as a "right," it is not received with gratitude or appreciation, and it becomes a burden to others. John's entitled attitude made him insensitive to the needs of others.

Love listens to fully help the speaker feel hear and to

understand them. Someone self-absorbed doesn't do this well. You can't care for others without sacrificing yourself for another, listening to them instead of just talking about yourself, affirming rather than retreating into your own thoughts.

John was my father. I chuckle every time I remember a family reunion where I hung out at a firepit in the backyard to keep warm and be away from Dad. A woman came rushing to the bonfire and said, "I just had to get away from *that* man." She went on to tell me about my father. His habit of demanding that others agree with him and talking down to people made her want to run away from him.

The battle to put energy into knowing and being known versus impressing or controlling others is one we all face daily. The irony is: the more we humble ourselves and honor others, the more we are filled with satisfaction, contentment, and joy. Only humble people are loving. Love requires humility. Love is sacrificial.

Discussion Questions:

What "rights" do you and your spouse have in your marriage?

How do entitled attitudes separate?

How does expecting love affect a family?

Prayer:

Lord, help me see my entitled attitudes and the ways I seek to impress others.

5:2

Fine Tuning

"For you know that we dealt with each of you as a father deals with his own children, encouraging, comforting and urging you to live lives worthy of God, who calls you into his kingdom and glory." 1 Thessalonians 2:11–12

Frank loved his video games. Abby, his wife, hadn't minded the new console in the living room—until she noticed over two-hundred dollars he'd paid that month online. He had agreed to cut back on spending to help reduce their debt. A sense of concern grew weeds in her heart.

How could he spend so much money without even telling me? She wondered if Frank would cut back even if she confronted him. What else could Frank be hiding? If he lacked self-control in buying, would he lack self-control when it came to pornography, prostitution, or a girlfriend on the side?

Abby knew productive discussions happened because of a gentle start. If she sounded accusing, Frank would be defensive, preventing communication and collaboration. Money supported the family, but trust supported their relationship. She prayed for him before they talked. It took courage, but Abby told Frank she felt frightened about their spending and asked him to review their budget with her. They used the evening talking about their spending: the power it had over them, how to be in control, and support each other.

Harmony doesn't come in a vacuum. Asking for God to guide us, submitting our own agenda to God, and gently asking our beloved for their help in resolving our concerns can bring harmony.

Discussion Questions:

When something is out of sync with you, how do you want your spouse to address it?

When are disagreements productive, and when do they become a rut of repeated phrases?

How do you resolve issues?

Prayer:

Lord, give me the strength to problem-solve issues that hinder love in our lives.

5:3

Imperfect Love—Imperfect Respect

"However, each one of you also must love his wife as he loves himself, and the wife must respect her husband." Ephesians 5:33

Arianna grimaced when her counselor asked her to name her husband's strengths. All she could think of was the messy, unorganized way he lived.

She sighed when the counselor then asked her how her husband showed love to her and listed a few ways.

The counselor leaned forward. "If you became disabled, do you think Ryan would still love and take care of you?"

"Not well," she said.

"So, his love is imperfect, but unconditional. Is your respect unconditional?"

"What? He has to EARN my respect!"

"Do you have to earn his love?" The counselor tapped his pencil for effect. "God requires men to *show* love to their wives as a gift to God and requires women to *show* respect to their husbands as a gift to God. Wives can be less than loveable, and husbands can be less than respectable, but giving love and respect shows honor. If we can't love or respect our teammates in our own power, we can love and respect God through our love to them. Love begets respect, and respect begets love, but even if nothing changes, we can still love and respect each other."

When Arianna began training herself to think about

Ryan's strengths, an important shift took place in their relationship. She had to think about what she said before she spoke, to make sure her words showed respect. After a while, she felt more respect for him, seeing his strength and integrity instead of camping out among his faults. And Ryan seemed to show her more love.

We all want to please those who see the best in us and hide from those who keep our faults in front of us. It takes effort to think about our words before we speak to ensure love and respect come out of our mouths, not the poisons of disrespect, sarcasm, contempt, or blame.

Discussion Questions:

What does "I love you" mean to you?

What behaviors and attitudes show respect to you?

How does it feel to you when you experience disrespect or a lack of love?

Prayer:

Lord, help me show my teammate love and respect.

5:4

Love—The Only Thing

"My command is this: Love each other as I have loved you. Greater love has no one than this: to lay down one's life for one's friends." John 15:12–13

Andrew noticed a car racing past him on the highway. Six-year-old Aiden in the back seat said, "Papa, don't let him pass you; he's going to win!"

Like Vince Lombardi who said, "Winning isn't everything; it's the *only* thing," we feel acceptance, applause, and value come from winning. In relationships if our winning makes someone else lose, winning isn't everything, it's the *lonely* thing.

We feel like we're losing when someone else seems to be winning an argument, so we turn the conversation to go down another road. There are many roads which will only lead to confusion and hurt, but we go down them anyway so we can feel we're winning. Changing the subject, bringing up the past, refusing to discuss a topic, blaming, intimidating with words, tone or voice, negative messages or even physically hurting someone are all ways we destroy harmony. Without thinking about what we're doing, we spiral a relationship down when we feel threatened.

Jesus flips our definition of what it means to "win." In John 15:12, Jesus calls us to love as *He* has loved. His flesh might have wanted to wipe out the vile Romans and save His country from oppression and humiliation, and shine as the conqueror, but His purpose wasn't to attain popularity nor conquests on earth. He submitted His ego to the Father. Instead, He served, laying down His life for His friends.

Discussion Questions:

When do you use tactics to change the direction of a problem-solving conversation?

How would it change your relationship if you both seek to serve each other?

What tactics do you sometimes use when in a heated discussion?

Prayer:

Lord, help me focus on serving rather than winning.

5:5

Falling From Grace

"Come to me, all who are weary and burdened, and I will give you rest." Matthew 11:28

When Andrew and I first married, fleeing conflict was my defense mechanism. Whenever I felt tension in our relationship, I reacted by running away. I'd take long walks, kick rocks and cry. Because I grew up with a critical father I could never please, I'd automatically assume that I wasn't measuring up with my husband's expectations of me. And when Andrew seemed upset, my childhood traumas set off daggers inside me. I now understand that the intensity of my reaction had more to do with my pain growing up than it did with Andrew's actions, and his reactions had more to do with his pain from a previous relationship than my actions.

Sometimes, we chaff against our teammates on a subconscious level because a past hurt has been triggered. We may not know why we or our spouse reacts (or over-reacts,) but that doesn't mean that we should just continue the way things are. Instead, we can patiently invite our teammate to explore their feelings of hurt and frustrations, trace them to their triggers, and we can do the same for ourselves. Identifying the true source of our irritations enables both parties to recognize and lovingly respond to them when conflict arises. Once we both feel heard and known, we can then problem-solve together to meet both of our needs.

I learned to try to take my emotional hurts from the present and past to offer them to God. When my beloved, Andrew, is hurting or angry, I pray for him and encourage him to lift his past hurts to God, as well.

We don't have to live with hurt and conflict alone. God is waiting to listen to our grief and bring healing into our lives.

Discussion Questions:

How do you tend to respond to conflict? What do you think is the root cause of that response?

What are some healthy ways you can work on any unresolved trauma from your past that you've unconsciously carried forward into your current relationship?

What are the advantages of letting God heal you?

Prayer:

Lord, heal our past hurts and give us the mercy and grace to love our sweetheart as they work through their own past hurts.

5:6

The Funny Faces Of Love

"There is a way that seems right to a man, but in the end it leads to death." Proverbs 14:12

Alexi talked fast telling her husband, Matt, why they needed a house instead of living in their shabby apartment. Matt stammered, unable to respond to her onslaught. Feeling overwhelmed, he wanted to hide, but he knew he couldn't escape.

Alexi hated when Matt ignored her, and she was determined to make her point clear, whether he wanted to hear it or not. Her words dripped with contempt as her voice got louder. She thought he deserved it.

In his book, *The Seven Principles that Make Relationships Work*, John Gottman reports that couples can survive having some negative behaviors in their marriage and remain happy, by using "repair attempts" where one partner signals that they need to take a break from the intensity of their fight and cool off. This can be done by make a joke, a funny face, or discussing waiting to continue the conversation at another time.

When an intense discussion raises blood pressure and one or both gets defensive, having the habit of making repairs may save your relationship. Each can pray about their needs, get hold of their negative patterns, try to communicate their needs using "I" statements, and have empathy for their partner. Once the tension has been released, then they can problem-solve.

According to Gottman, winning an argument can be devastating to the relationship when the other person feels they have lost. Poisons like sarcasm, contempt, giving the silent treatment, showing defensiveness, and being critical, destroy love and trust.

Alexi needed to help Matt express his feelings and thoughts so he wouldn't feel bullied. She had to learn to listen and draw out his opinions. Though she was gifted in being able to express her opinion, that strength became a fault in their relationship when Matt felt unheard and misunderstood.

Discussion Questions:

What behavior patterns hinder you from feeling heard in your relationship?

What can you do to prevent those poisons from building up and ruining your relationship?

What signal could you give your teammate to indicate that you need to take a step back and collect yourself?

Prayer:

Lord, help us show love when we're resolving conflicts.

5:7

Dragging My Briars

"A man reaps what he sows. The one who sows to please his sinful nature, from that nature will reap destruction; the one who sows to please the Spirit, from the Spirit will reap eternal life." Galatians 6:7-8

I wore a long dress as I ventured in the dark, moonless night to visit my mom a few hundred yards away. Slipping into the inky darkness of our country home, I felt the shape of the ground under my feet as I walked without a flashlight. A noise close by sent goosebumps up my arms. My heart raced. I stopped, and the rustling stopped. As I continued, the noise continued. Praying, I grabbed the back of my dress where the sound seemed to originate and discovered a long briar attached to the hem of my dress. I'd been dragging my noisemaker.

In the same way, we can drag briars in the form of attitudes and actions without knowing what hurt they will cause to those we are intending to love.

Nate used to go out drinking with the guys when he was young. The briars of drunkenness that hung on his friends seemed fun, and he wanted to have "fun" too. But as a result, his wife lost her admiration and trust in him, and became entrenched in bitterness from the many ways his drinking hurt her. That bitterness toward her husband rubbed off onto her sons who all went on to struggle with their identities as men.

Our darling can help us see our briars before they seed another generation. When our sweetie brings up an issue, we need to trust that they are bringing them to our attention because they care for us, not because they're trying to force change on us. Bringing our concerns to each other in a positive and gentle manner help free us from struggles we can't always identify on our own, and it can change our family's future.

Discussion Questions:

What tempts me to pursue something that feeds my flesh, or pride?

How can I help my spouse stay free of briars?

How do I want my spouse to help me with my briars?

Prayer:

Lord, help me be open to discussing my habits and attitudes with my sweetheart.

CHAPTER SIX: PROBLEM SOLVED!

6:1

Fickle or Faithful

"What a man desires is unfailing love; better to be poor than a liar." Proverbs 19:22

Jean and Will lived separate lives even though they were married. She worked hard at managing the house, kids, and her teaching career as did Will at his computer software job, keeping up the cars and yard, but there was no warmth between them. Jean slept as close to the edge of their king bed as she could. A friend commented on how distant they seemed to each other.

Patrick Lencioni's business book, *The Five Dysfunctions of a Team* has principles that apply to teammates in a relationship too. Taken from his overview, the absence of trust is the foundational reason for dysfunction. A lack of trust breeds a fear of conflict, leading to a lack of commitment.

Dysfunction played out in Jean and Will's relationship as Will's tendency to be easily irritable kept Jean from being able to trust that he would be kind. She stuffed her feelings to avoid conflict. Because issues then couldn't be resolved between them, commitment naturally waned.

Instead of focusing on Will, she looked for ways for her need to be valued, known and connected outside their relationship leaving her vulnerable.

Developing and sustaining deep trust is the core need of every team member. Problem-solving with someone you cherish begins with valuing each person's need to build trust, especially if trust has been broken in the past. Being trustworthy to show unfailing love is the first worthy goal a team member can have.

Discussion Questions:

On a scale of 1 to 10, with 10 being highest, what is the current trust level you have with your teammate?

Since trust is needed to problem-solve effectively, how can you increase the trust level between you?

Why do you think the proverb says that it is better to be poor than for your commitment to be proven false?

Prayer:

Lord, help us prioritize loving our teammate well.

6:2

Stuck

"Come to me, all you who are weary and burdened, and I will give you rest. Take my yoke upon you and learn from me, for I am gentle and humble in heart, and you will find rest for your souls. For my yoke is easy and my burden is light." Matthew 11:28-30

Carrie and Tom disagreed about how to raise their three wild kids. She wanted to be a tender but not a tough mom. After being disrespected long enough, she lost control and yelled at the kids. They ignored her since she never gave them consequences. Tom insisted she had to discipline them more. She admitted to not being consistent, but it was all too hard. Tom and Carrie fought about it all the time. He'd get mad and make kids pick up their messes, but Carrie would defend them and feel he wasn't being gentle enough.

They tried problem solving, but it always ended up with Carrie feeling like a failure, and Tom feeling helpless, and both being angry with neither understanding the other. Their emotions and conflict seemed to be forever swirling but never to touch down anywhere near land.

Sometimes we need outside help when our conflict becomes too difficult to handle on our own. Breakthrough for Carrie and Tom came when they sought help from qualified professionals. Carrie needed professional counseling to help her overcome her learned powerlessness.

The couple needed help with the children too. They read, *Parenting with Love and Logic*, and signed up for a Love and Logic parenting class. A woman from their church offered to help Carrie support new patterns in the home. Tom and Carrie held a family meeting and explained how they needed the children's help to create a healthy family. They laid out new rules and acknowledged that it wouldn't be easy. But Tom would support Carrie, and she in turn would allow him to be strong without being overbearing. Getting the help that they needed and making changes, made all the difference in their and their children's lives.

Discussion Questions:

How can brainstorming ideas to find solutions to your problems help you find answers you weren't aware of?

What are some reasons that people have for not reaching out for help from others?

What areas might you have that require some outside help to gain a new perspective? What prevents you from getting that help?

Prayer:

Lord, guide us to effective ways to solve our problems, even if we hadn't considered them before.

6:3

Cops And Robbers

"Therefore, judge nothing before its appointed time; wait till the Lord comes. He will bring to light what is hidden in darkness and will expose the motives of the heart. At that time each will receive their praise from God." 1 Corinthians 4:5

Did you ever play Cops and Robbers when you were young? One kid would be the robber who would "steal" and run, and the cop would give chase to get back what was lost. While not exactly the same, problem solving sometimes feels like a game of Cops and Robbers. For example, if I've overspent during the month and my husband says he wants to sit down to talk about the budget and our spending, I want to run and hide. Even if the money was spent on "necessary items" that we hadn't planned for, I still see myself as the selfish robber who spent all our money. I'm afraid Andrew might chase me down to put me in money jail.

It may seem silly, but there's always a logical reason for our emotional responses. In my case, I go back to a fear from my childhood, when Dad would yell and spank me anytime I stepped out of line. Even though I know that my emotional response to discussing the budget isn't logical, I still cower like that tiny girl in trouble again.

When my instinct to run and hide crops up, I need to remember that Andrew married me and all the hurts hiding inside me. Recalling the times in the past that he has given me grace when I messed up allows my mind to free itself from fight and flight so that I can sit down with my husband, and focus on our problem, not my behavior.

Having learned my response to trouble, Andrew has found ways that help prevent me from falling into old behavior patterns. When we need to have a serious talk, his body language isn't intimidating. He wears a gentle expression on his face. We use a notebook and write ideas down, examining our expenses and problem solving how much "mad" money we each get. No "Cops and Robbers" in our marriage anymore. Andrew's compassion has allowed me to build trust. He accepts me as a flawed human knowing that he also has flaws.

Discussion Questions:

Why do we judge each other?

What body language does your spouse see in you that makes problem solving difficult?

What do you want your precious spouse to say to you if your tone or body language is intimidating or frustrating to him or her?

Prayer:

Lord, since you are the only judge, free us to be teammates and step out of conflict by speaking the truth in love.

6:4

Quilting Our Trust

"The Lord detests lying lips, but he delights in people who are trustworthy." Proverbs 12:22

I love quilting, sewing scores of hand-picked fabrics with borders to set off designs. I sandwich the quilt top together with a batting, and a back, then I quilt them all together. It can take years to create a quilt. And when it rips, I make sure to repair it before it tears more.

Trust is like that. It is built when we follow through on our agreements and do what we say we will do. When we first get to know each other, we each try hard to look trustworthy. But as time goes by, we may have less motivation to maintain trust and don't follow through with our commitments. When that happens, there are rips in our trust quilt. The patterns that our sweetheart once admired doesn't quite align anymore. Hm. Other priorities come above our partner, or one takes the other for granted. It's easy focus on the other's mistakes and faults. When these things happen, trust gets torn because we pledged to love the other, and we're not.

In a relationship, we can keep cozy under that Trust Quilt. Building trust depends on honesty, kindness, and follow-through. Allowing each other to help us be accountable can help us both be the person we said we'd be. Our relationship will be as sweet as the trust we build.

Discussion Questions:

How's the trust between you?

What helps you trust each other?

What "rips" your trust?

Prayer:

Lord, let us live trusting you and building trust with our spouses.

6:5

Dreamers And Builders

"But the wisdom that comes from heaven is first of all pure; then peace-loving, considerate, submissive, full of mercy and good fruit, impartial and sincere." James 3:17

I am a dreamer. I like to share ideas and look for feedback. When we're talking and I present an idea, (ideas are dreams), I look for a yes, I agree, or no, I disagree response. Andrew on the other hand, is a builder. Where I have a picture in mind, he focuses on the details, which can confuse me when answers are vague and filled with qualifications. Here's an example:

I ask, "Do you want take in a matinee movie? It's at four o'clock and lasts a couple hours."

He replies, "Oh, I have an elder's meeting at seven. That only gives us a half-hour to eat."

"So, no going to the movie?" I am puzzled.

"Yes, I'd like to go if you can figure out what can be made and eaten in a half-hour."

Recognizing that different people have different ways of seeing life helps us avoid confusion and miscommunication. For instance, Dreamers have the big picture in mind. They want to know if we see their vision. But Builders want the specifications: how long will we be there? What will it cost? What else or who else needs consideration?

Before the Builder looks for specifications, it's a good idea for them to understand and affirm the Dream. The conversation might look something like this:

"What do you think about joining the Aquatic Center?

"Good idea! Let's work out the details over dinner."

What if one of us doesn't like the dream at all? We could still affirm the Dreamer - without affirming the dream. It could sound something like: "Honey, I like that you're looking for ways to keep us healthy and active. I don't share your passion for swimming but thank you for bringing ideas to the table."

Dreamers gets nowhere without Builders; Builders get nowhere without dreams. The ingredient that allows the two to blend are affirmation and patience.

Discussion Questions:

What dreams do you have that you'd like your honey to appreciate?

Choose a dream each of you has and decide how to build it.

How do your differing gifts help in building that dream into something tangible?

Prayer:

Lord, help us build dreams in harmony.

6:6

"Pet Projects"

"You, my brothers and sisters, were called to be free. But do not use your freedom to indulge the flesh; rather, serve one another humbly in love." Galatians 5:13

We each have areas, pet projects, around the home that we consider vitally important. Mine include the garden and house. Andrew has his own, but the yard isn't on his list. If I waited for him to mow the lawn, I'd wait for decades. Our yard isn't on his radar. If I chose to harp on him about the length of the grass, it could lead to a cycle of conflict that could result in a lifetime of blame, hurt and misunderstanding. When one partner feels more of the burden of household care than the other, they can negotiate ways to share the load and work together in a way that produces harmony without conflict or resentment.

Andrew and I are both busy with jobs outside the home, so I suggested he and I do one thing per day for the house or garden. He agreed, and we made a list to put on the refrigerator. Since he hates to mow the lawn, I give him other options that he might enjoy and that would bless me at the same time. Now, he's not the only one with free time on the weekends. He may not love my pet projects, but when I share with him what I need, he shows love to me by shouldering my burdens. And I in turn can do the same for him.

Discussion Questions:

What pet projects do you carry alone around your home?

Which projects do you need support to carry? What support do you need?

Make a list of each of your projects and pray over each, asking God for his perspective on them. Listen for new ideas and perspectives.

Prayer:

Lord, give us compassion for the concerns of our mate.

6:7

The Drama Virus

"Love your enemies and pray for those who persecute you". Matthew 5:44

Dr. Stephen Karpman developed the "drama triangle" to help patients understand that we tend to fall into one of three categories when we have conflict with others: the victim, the persecutor, or the rescuer. The roles shift depending our situation.

Here's an example: Brenda said to her husband, Tom, "Justin just lied to me, saying he went to all his classes, but the school's attendance secretary called at noon to say he missed his morning classes. You need to discipline him." From Brenda's perspective, she's the victim who has been lied to, Justin is the persecutor who has deceived her, and Tom is the rescuer who is bringing Justin to justice.

Tom went to Justin and said, "Son you lied to your mom, you're grounded for two weeks." From Justin's perspective, he feels like the victim who is being unfairly punished, and his dad is the persecutor, so he seeks a rescuer in his mother.

Justin complains to Brenda in the kitchen. She confronts her husband, "Tom, two weeks? Really? Don't you think that's harsh?"

Now Tom feels like he's the victim and Brenda is the persecutor, though she feels like she's the rescuer and Tom is the persecutor.

All three roles are enemies of harmony when used incorrectly. When we step into the role of persecutor without considering that there may be two sides to the story and lay down the law in anger or frustration, we pervert God's justice, which calls all of us to repentance. When we jump into a situation to try to "rescue" a victim from facing the consequences of their own folly, we risk usurping God's role as redeemer. And when we play the victim card, knowing that we are at fault (partially or fully) for the situation we find ourselves in, we act in defiance of God's discipline and call to repentance.

There is a time to discipline children, and a time to help those who can't help themselves with God's leading, but when judgment, self-importance, and feigned helplessness pull us into the roles of persecutor, rescuer and victim, we've left God behind.

Dr. Karpman's *Drama Triangle* is helpful in allowing us to recognize patterns in our behavior, but if we wish to break out of that vicious cycle of bickering and disharmony in our home, we first need to invite God back into the center of our homes and our conflict. Only then can we cut the drama and learn to speak the truth in love.

Discussion Questions:

When have you participated in the drama triangle?

How would it change the dynamics of your family if you all spoke the truth gently and loved each other more than yourselves?

How has God provided your needs in the past?

Prayer:

Lord, free us from seeing ourselves and each other as a victim, a persecutor, or a rescuer.

CHAPTER SEVEN: ADMIRING EACH OTHER'S DIFFERENCES

7:1

Iron to Iron

"As iron sharpens iron, so one person sharpens another." Proverbs 27:17

Iron sharpens iron through the force of grating friction. Those closest to us experience our most irritating tendencies and they experience ours. This can lead to friction in the home, yet differences also can be the tool needed to whittle away our impatience and imperfections. As Christians we are being formed into new creatures, and God often uses our teammate in that process. It isn't our opinions and rants that will survive the judgment fires at the end of days, it is our love. (1 John 4:16&17)

Our differences give opportunity for us to experience the sandpaper of change, and what we sacrifice in the name of love, sculpts us into something more beautiful than we could have imagined.

Andrew's energy level is much lower than mine. I've been high energy since I was born. I NEED to move. Sometimes he needs a nap. Accepting his need for rest has opened me to a more balanced view of what is important.

I see value in what is accomplished. He sees value in what is known. We both need to take our differences and see from God's perspective. Jesus said that Mary's focus on listening to Jesus was better than Martha's insistence that dinner be ready on time. That lesson wouldn't be in front of me continually if I were married to someone just like me.

Saying to God, "Thank you that Andrew is very different from me," paved the way for me to accept, enjoy and learn from him. I have lessened my hold on my favorite idol, "achievement," and have learned to balance my work with play because of him.

It's confusing to be confronted with differences, but with prayer and listening to your teammate, each person can become more understanding and more connected than before.

Discussion Questions:

What are some ways that you and your teammate are different?

How do those differences give you an opportunity to grow?

What would make your teammate feel loved the most? How can you make that happen?

Prayer:

Lord, give us wisdom to understand what is important when we're baffled with our differences.

7:2

Using The Right Oil

"If I give all I possess to the poor and surrender my body to the flames, but have not love, I gain nothing." I Corinthians 13:3

Cars must have oil to work. Without the lubrication provided by oil, parts will grind against each other down instead of gliding. A car with no oil creates friction. Eventually, it will seize up, the engine ruined. Showing care and appreciation in a relationship accomplishes what oil does for the car. It keeps the relationship running without friction and cleans us of the little resentments we build up.

The kind of oil matters too. For vehicles, a variety of oils suit the season and type of vehicle. There are ways to show love that match our mates more than others. In his book, *The 5 Love Languages: The Secret to Love that Lasts*, Gary Chapman, describes five ways of expressing love: gift giving, words of encouragement, acts of service (like washing their car for them), quality time (like a driving together to talk or enjoying dinner out), and touching (hugs, back scratches, hand-holding).

My love language is touching. If Andrew gave me a gift, told me how much he appreciated me, fixed something in the house for me or spent some quality time out to dinner with me, I would enjoy it. But I would still hunger to be held and not feel loved if he didn't give me non-sexual touches. When a spouse shows his sweetie love using *his own* favorite love language, he assumes she feels loved, but *his* favorite may not be *her* favorite and vice versa. Loving well means knowing and loving in the way your beloved wants to be loved.

Discussion Questions:

What is your favorite love language?

How specifically do you want to be loved in that way?

Rate the different ways of showing love according to what means the most to you.

Prayer:

Lord, show us how love each other well.

7:3

His Logic Bored A Hole In My Logic Board

"Do not be wise in your own eyes," Proverbs 3:7

I have an old Mac computer. My husband has a PC. When I get stuck with my computer, I ask him to help me, but he doesn't talk "Mac," and he usually has no idea how to get it to work. The laptops are different. Andrew and I are different in how we process things, too.

Sometimes my husband and I misunderstand each other. I talk to express my ideas. He talks to communicate information. He doesn't see the need to speak when no directions or information are needed. I speak to express my feelings or needs. I give hints about what I like and what I want. He doesn't understand, much less speak, "Hint."

He thinks I start helping him load the dishes because he's not doing it right, but I want to show him love by helping him.

When I'm playing the piano and he interrupts me to ask me a question, he thinks I can stop and start without losing my mind. He's wrong.

If I expect my husband to think the way I do or to speak the same way for the same reasons I speak, I'm sadly mistaken. And, I miss out on the opportunity to learn to see God's world from a different vantage point. God created both of us to interact with the world and with each other through different strengths, interests, and communication styles. Only by listening to each other with the intent to understand, will we discover the true depth of uniqueness in the person we married.

Discussion Questions:

How are you two different?

Do the differences help or hurt your family?

What can you do to mitigate the negative impact of those differences?

Prayer:

Lord, help us discover anew the miracle of our teammate.

7:4

Adaptability: Duct Tape Rules

"I try to please everybody in every way. For I am not seeking my own good but the good of many, so that they may be saved." 1 Corinthians 10:33

We love duct tape because of its adaptability. You can use it to make repairs, hold things in place, or make crafty things such as duct-tape wallets. When we're flexible and adaptable, God can use us in more ways too. 1 Corinthians 10:33 says Paul tried hard to adapt to different cultures and situations to love people better. It takes more patience to love some people than others. Everyone is different. For instance, when it comes to personal space—some people are huggers while others need more distance. Adaptability allows us to connect with more people, and it allows us to be closer to our sweetheart.

Andrew and I have different brains. Andrew has difficulty multi-tasking. I can juggle many levels of thought, jumping back and forth. If I jump topics when speaking to him, he gets lost and stuck.

As a result, I try to flex. My old pattern of blurting out what I wanted before I had his attention didn't work, so I've developed more self-control. Before I spontaneously interrupt him while he's working on his computer, I ask him if I can talk to him. He stops, focuses on me, and usually says "yes." This signals to me that I have his attention, and it signals to him that I respect him and his time.

Dr. Neil Clark Warren thought adaptability was so important that he said, "this (adaptability) may be the most important dimension of all." [3]

No couple has everything in common. We must adapt if we want to stick together. Intimacy is a dance of cooperation not based on my comfortability but on my commitment to love, which takes flexibility.

Discussion Questions:

When have you adapted to meet your partner's needs this past week?

In what area of your relationship would you like more adaptability from your partner?

How can your teammate affirm you in being adaptable?

Prayer:

Lord, help us be aware when we're rigid and ask you to help us develop adaptable love.

7:5

The Best Blend

"The greatest among you should be like the youngest, and the one who rules like the one who serves." Luke 22:26

Amanda used to resent her husband-Shawn's lack of organization. They wanted to take a vacation, but he wouldn't plan ahead where they would stay or what they would do which would leave her feeling frazzled and apprehensive instead of looking forward to the time away.

As God worked in her over time, she came to realize that Shawn had his own gifting, different from hers, but no less valuable. Now she plans vacations, and he reads to the kids and teaches them art and music. Shawn loves that Amanda's brain is linear; she thinks sequentially. His brain is random, making it hard for her to follow his logic at times. But, once they discovered more about each other and stopped judging each other, they learned to recognize their differences as strengths in their marriage. Their children benefit from Shawn's random free-thinking brain encouraging them to be creative and funny, and from Amanda's linear brain helping kids understand logic and consequences.

When we accept our differences, we stop saying: "That's not right. I know how it should be done." Instead, we learn to serve each other considering the other person's differences and needs. The divergent traits in us don't make either of us right or better, just better adapted for specific areas.

Discussion Questions:

Do you tend to think in a linear or random fashion?

How could your non-dominant thought process benefit your family?

If you value your gifting above your spouse's, how does that affect them?

Prayer:

Lord, help us honor our spouse's gifting.

For more information see:
Dr Anthony Gregorc, *Mind Style Models*

7:6

Ground Level

"For who regards you as superior? What do you have that you did not receive? I Corinthians 4:7 NAS

I'm so glad Andrew doesn't feel like he's more valuable because he's so smart. If he viewed himself as superior, without a word, he'd tell me every day that I don't measure up. Love's enemy is pride. I wish I could point fingers and say I never have pride, but it's a human condition, like a disease that needs a watchful eye and a quick remedy. Here's how I visualize pride. If I stay ground level, not elevating myself (arrow up) nor diminishing my value (arrow down) I can protect myself from the lies of pride.

A belief that I'm more valuable than others is a lie that robs closeness because it erects a nonverbal rejection notice directed to anyone "lesser than me" in my eyes. Thus, a person I feel superior to is robbed of feeling appreciated and loved. The proud one is robbed of intimacy because with a rise in his perceived status comes the need to defend oneself against anything which would challenge that status.

Since none of us is better than everyone else in every area, we resort to fault-finding, fear of exposure, ingratitude, neglect of others, inability to see truly, entitlement, defensiveness, attention seeking and so on in order to feed our need to rise above others. My enemy becomes myself because I have flaws and shame I now want to hide. I create a war both within me and between me and others in order to maintain my status of being better than others.

The arrow down represents things I'm ashamed of and want to keep hidden from others. I've judged myself as worse than others by comparing myself to people. It's reverse pride.

By receiving God's grace and perspective, the areas I've judged in myself can be healed. Then I have nothing to hide and can share myself. True intimacy can only happen with humility.

Some people refuse to accept parts of themselves because they want more. Instead of making them better, the seeds of anger and its sister, depression, sap the self-worth of its owners. Understanding God's grace sets us free to accept ourselves as flawed but infinitely precious and capable, which in enables us to extend grace to other imperfect people and ourselves.

When I let go of the thinking that who I am or what I do makes me more or less valuable than others, I can live without having anything to prove or hide. I can be in the place capable of knowing others and being known without barriers. I can connect with God more fully in this place too, the place of acceptance and love for me, others, and God.

Discussion Questions:

How does pride hurt your relationship with your teammate?

How would having nothing to prove and nothing to hide facilitate intimacy?

How could this principle help your life and relationship?

Prayer:

Lord, enable us to have nothing to prove and nothing to hide.

7:7

Make The Sparks Fly

"Love is patient, love is kind. It does not envy, it does not boast, it is not proud. It is not rude, it is not self-seeking..." I Corinthians 13:4-5

Tucker told his wife jokingly, "I told you I loved you when we got married. If anything changes, I'll let you know." Never telling or showing his wife love would corrode the relationship like never changing or cleaning the spark plugs in his truck and expect it to run for three-hundred thousand miles.

Spark plugs need replacing from time to time. They get dirty, worn down, and corroded. If they aren't changed when they're worn out, your car might not start. Even if it does start, you'd be spending more money on gas because your car isn't burning fuel effectively. Left too long and you burn out your entire exhaust system. Spark plugs, like areas in our relationships, need new approaches and attitudes when the old ones make our relationship misfire. Our relationships corrode without ongoing love.

Our spouses need to feel loved, important, known, and treasured. The right amount of closeness and humility is necessary to create a spark.

Paul tells us in 1 Corinthians 13 how to love. Be patient with each other. Show kindness in all things. Don't live for your own ego or self-gratification, but to love.

John loved his job, and time flew when he worked. His

wife texted asking when he'd be home for dinner. She needed to spend time with and feel close to him. He had to choose to create sparks for his wife and not work late. If work was more important than her need to be connected to him, they'd lose the spark in their relationship.

Like the spark plugs which get dirty from use over time, our stinky and indulgent habits cause dirt to build up in our relationships too. They're like carbon on the spark plugs; they block love.

Different people need different activities to create excitement so that their relationship "sparks." Jason loved to bike with his wife. Pam liked to watch movies together with her husband. Justin wanted to have a regular date night. Karen wanted to go out dancing. Sam loved when he and his sweetie became involved in community theatre. When we look for ways to connect with each other through activities that we can both enjoy, we provide the maintenance necessary to keep the flame of our love burning bright and clear. Keep "sparking."

Discussion Questions

What sparks feelings of being seen and loved for your teammate? Ask them.

When do they sacrifice for you, so you feel loved?

How does kindness affect a relationship?

Prayer:

Lord, help us love generously with our time, effort, and imagination.

CHAPTER EIGHT: CULTIVATING INTIMACY

8:1

Beep for Better

"Live in peace with each other." 1 Thessalonians 5:13

I was driving home from church, and the rain clouds poured down onto my car on the I-5 freeway faster than my windshield wipers could swish the water away. Spray from a truck's tires distorted my view like a plunge into the sea as I drove fifty-miles-an-hour across a bridge. During the swoosh of a water, I had traveled into the lane on my left. The car coming up beside me beeped, alerting me to the danger we were in, and I jerked my wheel back so that I'd be in my own lane again.

Boundaries help guard and protect us in life and in relationships. It's important to have them. It's especially important in our closest relationships, especially in the area of sex. If we're not communicating our wants and needs, it's impossible for our partner to see where we're going. Without that visibility, they'll crash through our boundaries and both of us will end up hurt.

We need to give a friendly "honk" at each other if a teammate is doing something we don't like. If we blare our horns, we risk causing them to overcorrect and potentially harm the relationship even more. You know the difference between a beep and a prolonged honk. A beep might be a hint or a gentle. "Let's put on some music and take it slow." A horn blare might be something like, "You always have an excuse not to come to bed with me. You're just avoiding me."

Using statements that start with "I feel..." without any accusations, when we see our teammate coming into our lane and breaking through our barriers prevents crashes in the relationship. For instance, after noticing their teammates garlic breath, one can say, "I would love it if you brushed all that wonderful garlic off your teeth before kissing me tonight." Or for something more serious, "I feel rejected when I go upstairs and lay alone in bed until I fall asleep." (There is no "you" in the statement, so it doesn't raise the other's defenses.)

Sex is two individual journeys combining for the gratification of each other. Since everyone has their own experience, each must listen to the other how the journey should go. We all need to understand that the desires and feelings of one aren't the same as the other. Each has their own wishes for the frequency and process of it.

Healthy sex requires open, loving conversation to problem solve every issue. Don't forget to "beep".

Discussion Questions:

What are the issues you'd like to talk over about your sex life, but feel afraid to?

What about sex with your partner do you enjoy? What could be improved?

How would learning to communicate more effectively keep resentment or fear from building?

Prayer:

Lord, help us problem-solve our needs. Bring us harmony and mutual satisfaction.

8:2

Building A Nest

"Therefore, as God's chosen people, holy and dearly loved, clothe yourselves with compassion, kindness, humility, gentleness and patience." Colossians 3:12

My mother loved to drop wisps of cotton off her deck in the early spring. The sparrows dove and rose to catch the cotton in their beaks and carry it off to their nests. One male built several nests to woo his favorite female.

I don't know what characteristics birds look for when choosing a mate, but for humans, statistics state that most people choose their partners based on appearance and "chemistry." According to psychologist and writer, Neil Clark Warren, most of that (75-80%) disappears within six to eight months, unless there is a meaningful relational connection. [4]

How does one build a comfortable "nest" with a meaningful connection when wooing a mate? The tit for tat—"you do this for me, and then I'll do this for you" exchange people often expect is different from the unconditional love Christ calls us to give our teammate.

While it hasn't always been the case for Andrew and I in the past, growing in God's love, discipline and humility has allowed us to be in a loving relationship with each other. When talking about how to show love to others, Apostle Paul doesn't just *suggest* the Colossians clothe themselves with compassions, kindness, humility, gentleness and patience—he *tells* them to.

Not surprisingly, kindness is one of the top requirements for those over forty looking for a mate. Kindness emulates politeness, patience, and giving. That's how a soft nest is built. The rocks of pride, selfishness, over-control, harshness, and impatience make a painful roost, but a "nest" woven with kindness makes for a soft landing. Happy flying!

Discussion Questions:

How many kind actions did your spouse do for you today? What did it mean to you?

How happy are you with your love nest?

What could each of you do to make your nest warmer and softer?

Prayer:

Lord, show us how to build kindness into our relationship. Guide us in building a safe, warm, and lasting nest.

8:3

Fake Love

"But I tell you that anyone who looks at a woman lustfully has already committed adultery with her in his heart." Matthew 5:28

Ned had been procuring porn since junior high. It offered the excitement and comfort he longed for without vulnerability. Though he suspected porn controlled him, molding attitudes and beliefs which oppose love, he liked the fantasy and sense of control. However, because of it, he carried too much shame to be honest and open with his wife, so he developed a false front. This prevented real intimacy—and made it impossible for him to know her heart and let her know his heart. As a result, his offering of false love left her feeling unknown, unloved, and used.

Our obsession with separating sex from relationship has far-reaching effects on our culture and families. A lawyer I spoke with said nine out of the last ten divorces she'd handled were because of porn. Samantha Gallo wrote in her online article "The Effect of Pornography on Families" that porn rewires its user's brains, making them less satisfied with real sex. Usage also erodes empathy and fosters deep isolation, changing attitudes toward one's self and toward women in general.[5]

God created sex as one of many ways to share intimacy with the spouse who pledged their life in marriage to love you for a lifetime. Sex within a committed relationship of openness, respect and love (Biblical marriage), has as its goal the fulfillment of one's partner. Love is other focused, while porn is self-focused. Porn is the adultery of fantasizing about someone other than your spouse to create sexual release. It's the polar opposite of the selflessness of committed love.

Ned didn't want to give up his pornography. He enjoyed it. When his wife gave him an ultimatum: porn or me, he chose to join a *Celebrate Recovery* group and began the trek back to love. He found a friend to hold him accountable. He had to choose committed love over fantasy, to break his addiction. Instead of the emptiness of fake love, he learned to know and be known.

Discussion Questions:

How is pornography different from committed lovemaking?

Is pornography a temptation for you?

How tempting is pornography for you? If it is not tempting or not very tempting, to what do you attribute that?

Prayer:

Lord guide us to fill ourselves with genuine love and convict us when we seek fake love.

8:4

Intimacy

"Each one of you also must love his wife as he loves himself, and the wife must respect her husband." Ephesians 6:33

A friend of mine, Al, is a married-single man. Though married, he lives as a single person, baffled that his wife doesn't feel loved. Al brings home a paycheck and completes repairs on the house saying, "Whatever she needs done, I do." He's reliable, but his wife's love meter registers empty. He doesn't comprehend that a Biblical marriage is a mutual sharing of your heart, your body and your mind. He's often gone in the evening and never asks his wife how she is, what she thinks, or how she feels. Neither does he share his own feelings. Carol, his wife, struggles with suicidal thoughts—due to being trapped in feelings of being unknown and unloved.

There are many strands of intimacy:

1. Intellectual intimacy - that of thinking together
2. Social intimacy - enjoying other people together
3. Aesthetic intimacy - enjoying beauty together
4. Emotional intimacy - sharing your feelings, dreams, and past
5. Sexual intimacy - meeting both of your sexual needs
6. Spiritual intimacy - sharing your faith and appreciating each person's spiritual gifts
7. Physical intimacy - sharing housing tasks, shopping,

feeding and recreational activities

8. Affectional Intimacy-showing affection with non-sexual touch, words, gifts, acts and spending time together

The quality and quantity of connectedness in your relationship determines your sense of feeling loved and bonded. Each area impacts our feelings of closeness which impacts every other area. Intimacy's weaving of these strands requires communication, since we all have preferences which help us *feel* loved.

Discussion Questions:

Which of these intimacy strands do you wish were stronger? Which of these does your partner wish were stronger?

How can you strengthen them?

What will be the outcome if you grow your relationship to be a close, trusting, satisfying one?

Prayer:

Lord, show us how to be "one."

8:5

Arms Of Love

"He gathers the lambs in his arms and carries them close to his heart" Isaiah 40:11

I used to pretend to I was tough because I felt so vulnerable. Without a loving father, hunger to be held, known, and loved, pulsed through me as constant as my blood. God brought Andrew and me together and love bloomed. Andrew's arms holding me were from God's heart. The Holy Spirit doesn't have physical arms to hold me, but Andrew's arms are God's way to love me. I'm God's little girl.

My hands, likewise, are the gifts from God to love Andrew. Every time I rub his back, kiss the bald spot on his head, or make love to him, God is pleased with me loving his treasured son. We please God when we love.

A father can think about how he wants his little girl's husband to treat her. That's how God feels. A mother can consider what kind of woman she would want her son to marry and be that kind of woman in turn, because her husband is God's son.

A friend of mine made a sarcastic remark to her husband and then said she could treat him that way because he was her husband. But God treasures us and our spouses beyond what we could imagine. Our spouse is not our possession, but God's, which makes them worthy of great respect.

Andrew's primary love language is touching, and still I'm amazed when I see him relax and sigh when I simply touch his shoulder. As much as we need food for our body, we need love for our spirits.

Discussion Questions:

How do you want your spouse to show you he or she cares?

What impedes your affection for your partner?

How open are you to healing the wounds that prevent love's flow in you? What can you do this week to love more?

Prayer:

Lord, help me be your arms of love.

8:6

Exclusive Love

"My beloved is mine and I am his;" Song of Songs 2:16

From the time of my early childhood, I knew my father was having affairs. Growing up in a home with an unfaithful father resulted in me struggling to trust men all my life. After a stressful week attending my dying mother in the hospital, I went in to clean our guest bathroom and found the pair of thong underwear on the floor. I imagined a woman coming to our house and having sex with my husband. I'd been gone all week. It would have been easy. Shaken and sleepless, I asked my husband, Andrew, about it.

He denied any association to the underwear but wasn't defensive. He never said, "just trust me," but knowing how important trust is, welcomed me to check his phone and computer any time. He insisted we call each of the many houseguests who had visited us over the summer to find the owner.

I called every female who had stayed at our house and none of them claimed the underwear. I sobbed in Andrew's arms, and he supported me in my pain and confusion. I knew I couldn't trust my feelings either way; feelings are no indicator of truth. Andrew said he'd be willing to take a lie detector test. Trust was more important to him than the cost of the test.

Then, desperate to find any clues, he looked up the

brand name and discovered they were men's underwear. I called a male house guest who acknowledged they were his! Our friend had felt too embarrassed to ask me about them after realizing he'd left them behind.

Trust is everything in a relationship. My world shook because of my past experiences with people who cheated. I didn't know if I could trust my husband. We needed to build and maintain trust with openness and love. Because Andrew neither put up defenses, nor put me down, instead understood my need to have a foundation for trust, my trust in him and appreciation for him grew even more. To pursue love, we must establish and maintain trust.

Discussion Questions:

Why does trust matter?

What causes you to wonder if your spouse is faithful (physically, emotionally, mentally, financially)?

What can you do to confront that distrust to build a foundation of trust between you?

Prayer:

Lord, help us be faithful to our sweetie and maintain a foundation of trustworthiness for them.

8:7

Working At Love

"Better is a patient man than a warrior." Proverbs 16:32

I admire Pastor Dale Ebel for his openness in talking about sex from the pulpit. He told his congregation that he works harder to please his wife sexually than in any other area.

In the artificial world of media, we have watched uncountable love scenes. Make-up artists paint women to look stunning and sexy, even as they wake up, or get in a mud fight. People believe the lies portrayed in media that lovers always look beautiful—and never struggle or work to bring their spouse fulfillment. Yet in real life, no one looks stunning all the time and making love requires communication to develop the needed skills.

When Andrew plays his guitar and sings, I join him by playing the keyboard and singing harmony, but we must listen to each other to sound beautiful. Andrew's guitar needs to be tuned to match the keyboard. I work to make my harmony compliment his singing. We practice together until the sound is right. Without constantly listening to the other, our timing, our pitches, and sound aren't pleasing. Individuals need to listen to each other about the other's body as well. In every area, love requires communication, effort, and patience.

An old Anglican wedding vow says, "With this ring, I thee wed, with my body I thee worship." Traditional Christian marriage raised the bar on lovemaking to worship, referring to *worship* as a verb—to bring great honor, respect and reverence for your spouse in your bedroom.

Discussion Questions:

What does lovemaking mean to you?

What can your teammate do to make it more special?

What would it mean to you to worship your beloved with your body?

Prayer:

Lord, thank you for the opportunity to love my spouse with my body.

CHAPTER NINE: GOALS AND BEYOND

9:1

Little Piles

"Now to him who is able to do immeasurably more than all we ask or imagine, according to his power that is at work within us, to him be glory." Ephesians 3:20, 21

As I move around the house cleaning on my treasured days off from work, I find it's easy to move piles or make piles instead eliminating them. Throwing away trash, finding the right place for everything else, feels like a heavy task. Each item needs a decision. I have a cubby underneath a cabinet. It's a perfect place to throw items I don't want to deal with at the moment. But stashing those items away solves nothing. Instead, it compounds—and further complicates the mess when I finally am forced to sit down and face it.

We have places in our marriages we don't want to face too. We "shelve" conflict because it involves deciding. We put off creating a budget, making a will, figuring out a way to make a major repair, deciding about the kids, figuring out a date night (which might involve a sitter), because we see those decisions as a drain on our energy and joy when we're too tired to think.

Like that stashed stack of papers, the decisions pile up until we reach a point where we either face them or become crushed by them.

I've started a new thing when I see my pile. I pray—"God, I feel powerless to make the needed decisions to put these things in their rightful place. Give me the power and wisdom to do this." Then, in faith, I pick up the first piece and listen to God and decide what to do with it. It helps!

God is there for you and your teammate too. You don't need all the answers. You can pray and problem solve together until an answer is clear. Sometimes, wise counsel from an outside source may help. Whatever is in your pile, you don't have to face it alone. God, who created the universe is waiting for you to ask for help.

Once you don't feel buried under any piles, you may even discover you look forward to planning a new adventure with your sweetheart.

Discussion Questions:

What in your marriage pile is frustrating to you? What is it about those decisions that feel overwhelming to you?

What do you think is in your teammate's pile that is weighting them down? Ask them. Were you right?

How can you help each other?

Prayer:

Lord, give us the confidence to face our "piles," to pray over them, set goals with our spouse and watch you empower us.

9:2

Get Green

"Whoever sows sparingly will also read sparingly, and whoever sows generously will also reap generously." 2 Corinthians 9:6

When I peruse my garden, I'm guaranteed of only seeing crops that have been seeded into the soil. I plan my garden, planting seeds according to their needs for space, water, and light. Some plants help others. For instance, because of their offensive smell to bugs, I plant marigolds in areas I want to discourage insects from eating my crops.

My honey and I can plant seeds of harmony and excitement in our marriage. We consider the factors, time, expense, energy requirements, and how the overall family would be affected. We can brainstorm what seeds could be paired for the best outcome, and which seeds need more resources than we have.

Here's our plan: we read profound non-fiction books to each other before bed. This flowers in something interesting to talk about, time away from media facilitating better sleep, wisdom to absorb and good modeling for children to see. Another is walking in the morning with Andrew's mother. This will give us both exercise and a way to connect with Mom every day. A third seed is to take turns planning a date night once a week. That way both of us can have choices.

These seeds need tending and protecting. After we see

the seeds growing in the garden of our relationship, we can evaluate whether we have room for more seeds, or if we need to dig out what doesn't work for us.

My biggest garden destroyers are slugs and snails. I've learned to grab a flashlight and don a rubber glove just before bedtime to bag the buggers. Attitudes like self-pity, ingratitude and a critical spirit can destroy more growth than your relationship garden can grow. It takes a conscious effort to recognize these love suckers and bag them.

If we want *a lot* of fruit in our relationship, we need to feed the seeds with time, attention, affirmation, affection, problem solving, looking for conflict your teammate feels but doesn't want to tell you, and communicating well.

Grow great crops of love by seeding your life intentionally with activities that will yield the crops you want. Have adventures. Cultivate love.

Discussion Questions:

What kind of relationship do you want with your sweetie?

What actions can you take to make that happen?

What seeds will you plant this week to make that dream a reality?

Prayer:

Lord, wake us to see the love you want us to give to each other.

9:3

Separatists

"Choose for yourself this day who you will serve." Joshua 24:15

Sin doesn't result from separation from God—our sin *is a choice* that separates us from God. One choice at a time, each thought or action—expands the distance between us and God, saying: "I want what I want, when I want it—I don't care what you want, God." Or our choices, thoughts and actions can draw us near to God as we pray, listen to God, and submit to what we know is right and loving.

Likewise, every choice to ignore the needs of our spouse and indulge ourselves is a separation. Choosing to stay late at work when dinner is waiting, pulling out cereal for the family dinner when you had the resources to cook, clicking on a porn site, or nursing my grudge instead of using "I" statements to speak the truth in love—all result in separation.

A miracle happens when we walk in a relationship with God and ask him to show us how to love our spouse. Like my student who told me, "You always make me do things I can't do!" God takes time to mold us into who we could not be without Him, choice by choice, day by day as we listen and follow God.

Every choice we make results in a separation or closeness. Choosing love instead of pettiness, selflessness instead of selfishness, gentleness instead of stubbornness can bring us into a relationship with our spouse (and our Heavenly Father) beyond what we thought we could have.

Discussion Questions:

What choices do you make that separates you from your teammate?

What makes you feel separated more from your teammate?

How would you like your teammate to include you in their life? How can you be more inclusive of your spouse in your life?

Prayer:

Lord, help us love intentionally and to choose closeness instead of separation each day.

9:4

More Two-Gather

"Forgetting what is behind and straining toward what is ahead, I press on toward the goal to win the prize for which God has called me heavenward in Christ Jesus." Philippians 3:13-14

Ali and Norm Hansen dreamed of changing the world. They prayed for God to give them the vision He had purposed for them. They became Sunday School teachers together for a class of middle school children. Every day they prayed for each member of their class and held special events for their students. Samantha, a sixth grader, became serious about her faith as a result. She went on to affect the world with her books.

Just as earthly parents have dreams for their children, so Father God knows how His children can share their gifts, build each other up, bloom, and open their arms to others. Some of Hansen's friends are further examples of this—some became foster parents while others started a neighborhood support group for single moms. Another couple at church mentors an at-risk teen boy. Each life touched is altered for eternity. Every life changed affects every generation that proceeds from them. A life has many ripples, sometimes unseen until eternity. Pursuing these dreams together enriches each of these couples with purpose, fulfillment, and changes the world.

Ask God to show you His dream for you. It might be

a dream your teammate has understood already but has been waiting for you to be ready to take the first step with them. If your vision is hampered with doubt or defeat, remember, God has the power to make His dreams come true. Gather God's promises, and with prayer, ask for His vision and listen to Him. When you know your calling, fears and obstacles become problems for God to solve instead of being troubles for you to escape from. If you want what's supernatural, ask our supernatural God to lead you and follow Him. You don't have to do it all yourself. God unfolds dreams and gives us experiences, training, wisdom, and power as you step out in faith to love.

Discussion Questions:

What holds you back from pursuing the dreams God has placed in your life?

If you don't know what those dreams are, ask God, "What dreams do you have for us?" (Much like a trusted friend.) What did He tell you? What can you do to implement His response?

After you die, how do you want to be remembered by those who knew you? Do you want to write it down to help solidify it in your mind?

Prayer:

Lord, give us the courage to step into faith and press forward together in the work to which you have called us.

9:5

Change

"For it is God who works in you both to will and to act according to his good purpose." Philippians 2:13

Andrew and I both need to take vitamins, so we have a dispenser with little compartments for each day of the week. Sometimes, we can't remember that we've taken them and can look at the case. When the cubby is empty, we can move on. If the vitamins are still there, we know we need to take a moment to care for ourselves a little better. Now, if we just had a cubby that held the daily actions for working toward our new couple goals, our relationship might grow sweeter.

Ah, but we can! By setting a regular time to check in with each other, we can see how we're doing and renegotiate if we need to. Making communication a game, even with a reward, makes it fun. Offering words of encouragement and suggestions for problem solving any glitches in the process supports the changes you're working toward.

As a couple, we lead a small group Bible study and support group. On the refrigerator, we post the component tasks: study the text for the study, pray for the members, and call everyone to check in when needed. Andrew and I plan who will do each task and check it off when it's done. That way we both know that everything has been taken care of by the time we gather next.

We both want to lose weight, so we make it a game.

Every Saturday morning, we can both get on the scales. The one who lost the most gives the other a full-body massage that night.

Change takes bucking old behaviors and redirecting thoughts to form new habits (Romans 12:1-2). It's work! To change, we check in with each other often, and we also build in accountability, encouragement, and rewards.

Set yourselves up for success, plan and document your goals, and make the baby steps easy to do, easy to see if it's done, and easy to change when needed. Then reward each other!

Discussion Questions:

What are your two most important goals as a couple?

What support and accountability can you develop to make sure you make progress?

How can you renegotiate without negativity when you're not making the progress you want?

Prayer:

Lord, since you give us the desire and power to do what you want, help us walk with you to carry out your will in our lives and our marriage.

9:6

Comfort Zone

"Dear children, let us not love with words or tongue but with actions and in truth." I John 3:18

As I write this, the world is going through the COVID-19 pandemic. Among other fears, some of my friends and family are concerned that unemployment benefits will cause people to stay on unemployment, making it hard for the government to support people who could return to work. In seasons of extreme stress and uncertainty, it's more comfortable to stay home and do nothing.

In our relationships, it's easy to find a comfortable place and stay there too. Leroy worked his eight hours every weekday, and he expected his wife to have dinner ready and the house cleaned—even though she worked full time too. He'd worked hard all day. It was comfortable to insist she do the housework and uncomfortable listening to her complain about it.

Amy found it comfortable to watch a movie while they ate dinner, even though the family wanted to eat early and then go for a bike ride on a nearby bike path during warm summer evenings.

If we want to rise to fulfill God's vision for our lives, we must leave our comfort zone. No one accomplishes noble things if they never get out of bed. If we want splendid relationships, we must go through the uncomfortable places to build them. In every uncomfortable discussion and decision, God is with us and can guide us. Our relationship grows stronger every time leave our comfort zone to understand and show care to each other.

Discussion Questions:

What kind of life does a person live when comfort is the most important thing to them?

What kind of life do you want to live?

What is one "uncomfortable" thing you can do this week to show care for your spouse?

Prayer:

Lord, give us perspective when we want to live for comfortability instead of purpose.

9:7

Success

"Love never fails." 1 Corinthians 13:8

Just before COVID hit, we met a homeless guy at church, and after the service, we took him to dinner at a local restaurant. While we were talking, I asked him what he wanted to do in life. He replied, "I want to succeed." When I asked what kind of job he wanted, he said he didn't know, nor did he know how he could "succeed." The desire was there, but he lacked a roadmap and a compass, so he did not understand where to begin.

Many people don't know how to succeed in relationships either. They have the desire to have a successful relationship that is meaningful and fulfilling, but they often lack examples of what successful relationships look like—which makes it difficult to determine how to begin one.

In my twenties, a guy wanted to date me because I had blond hair. Because of the world he grew up in, he believed marrying a blond would signify success. He had no clue there was more to relationships than hair color and body types. Hollywood has raised generations of adults to believe that love is a feeling you get when you meet someone who looks like a movie star, not a relationship you build with a real person. To succeed, you must be willing to do the hard work. And you must be willing to accept, success doesn't come without mistakes and failures.

For Andrew and me, success means loving each other

well, fanning the flames of each other's gifting and passions. But we've also learned that we have to deal with the hard things inside our own hearts to love each other well.

You too can create your own unique journey of love, cooperation, intimacy, and enjoyment of each other. Decide together what "succeeding" means in your relationship. Discuss how you'll respond to disappointments and failures. And how you can come alongside your spouse to help pick them up and dust them off when they fall short of success.

Discussion Questions:

What does a successful marriage look like to you? What skills do you need to develop or improve on to achieve the vision for your marriage?

What things (expectations, misconceptions, habits, etc.) are hindering you from having a successful marriage?

What is one thing you and your spouse can focus on developing or replacing in your marriage this week that will contribute to your relationship's long-term success?

Prayer:

Lord, show us your vision for our relationship. Give us the courage and humility to pursue it.

CONGRATULATIONS!

You've spent a lot of time deepening your relationship. It is my prayer that your relationship has grown immensely, that your dreams are coming true, and you'll model for your children and community a positive way of communicating and problem-solving which will create ripples of love and respect through generations. May you always seek God, and may His overwhelming love and grace fill your every day.

Contact us through barbararicewrites@gmail.com to let us know what you think or to join our email friend team. Check out our website at barbararicewrites.com for upcoming books and blogs.

We are Marriage Coaches for MarriageTeam. If you would like individual coaching that is focused on developing and applying enhanced relationship skills, then MarriageTeam coaching may be right for you.

Your Christian coaches will work with you and your spouse to help you apply the concepts in this book to resolve issues and grow closer to one another and the Lord. Your coaches will meet you where you are and help you get to where you want to be. They will help you tune-up whatever vehicle you are in, so it runs like a sports car. Your coaches have had their share of clunkers in the past and know what it is like to struggle in their relationship. They, like you, are on a journey and have their share of breakdowns. The only difference is that they a repair kit full of tools that they have been trained to use so they can get back on their journey much quicker than before. Your coaches will not give you advice, but help you figure out what is best for you, your relationship, and your journey together.

We speak from experience. MarriageTeam coaching significantly enhanced our relationship and provided the oil we needed to have a better running marriage. We trust the MarriageTeam coaching process and believe that you can too. Mention the book, *Tune-Up Your Relationship* for a discount on coaching.

To get a coach couple or for more information, check out www.marriageteam.org, email info@marriageteam.org or simply call 866 831-4201.

WHY DOES MARRIAGE MATTER?

When you marry, you stand up in front of your family and friends and pledge your love to your betrothed. Vowing to love each other well until one of you dies—that builds trust. Doing it in front of your community builds accountability and commitment. Committed love has a better foundation on which to build a stable relationship.

The idea of love and loving without manipulation or selfishness came from God. He wants both women and men to protect their hearts by making wise decisions regarding who and how they love.

Statistics show couples living together separated five times more often than married couples and had poorer relationships.[6]

Marriage isn't simply making vows; it's living them out decade after decade. Making a lifetime commitment points you in the direction of resolving conflict, rather than finding a new person and starting over again when developing harmony becomes difficult. It is hard at times. In this, the most intimate and revealing of relationships, your ego will be purified on the altar of love, or love will be sacrificed on the altar of your ego. Marriage isn't a state of having said the vows, marriage is the state where each person lives out their vows.

It's possible to express a deep loving commitment with your own private vows. But who doesn't want to throw a party and tell everyone in your tribe that you have found the love of your life? That's marriage. The fact that it's hard at times, and others have failed doesn't mean that it's not the best pathway to lifetime love.

WHY DOES GOD MATTER?

Andrew and I have a close and satisfying relationship, but even more intimate than our connection to each other is our relationship with God. He is our best friend. Daily time with God refreshes us, motivates us, and empowers us to love each other more wisely and deeply. Both Andrew and I want God to be first in our lives, so we prioritize Him. He calls us to honest communication. He calls us to surrender our anger. He calls us to forgive when we'd rather nurse our grievances. He calls us to be peacemakers.

Because God is the creator, author, designer, He is the one who defines us. He knows who we are and what we've done and who we can be. He knows our pain and feels our hurts since Jesus came to earth, lived, and suffered as a human, was crucified, and rose to life.

We were all made to be personally connected to God, perfectly loved, completely understood, and utterly treasured. Our estrangement from God leaves us with longing we try to fill. Attention seeking, sex, man's approval, alcohol, drugs, fame, money, prestige, power, the offenses of others all can own us, which is why most addiction counseling starts with surrender to your higher power. I love God when I see who He is, not only the all-powerful creator but a kind and gentle father. When I let God love me, I'm not desperate and can love others from a full heart.

RESOURCES

MarriageTeam coaching—www.MarriageTeam.org
MarriageTeam coach couples are trained volunteers. Most couples meet for eight to twelve weeks developing tools to enhance their own relationship. Usually, there is a $200 charge for the material and an on-line survey.

Coalition for Marriage, Families and Couples Education: http://www.smartmarriages.com
Classes, conferences, books, media information and other resources are available on their website.

Individual or couple counseling.
Check in your area for counselors.

Retreats and conferences.
Marriage Encounter: http://www.wwme.org
Focus on the Family: www.focusonthefamily.org>marriage
Family Life Seminars: www.familylife.com
Love & Respect: www.loveandrespect.com

Mentor Couples: ask your local church to help you find a mentor couple.

NEW BOOKS BY BARBARA RICE

During the fall of 2020, *Cry of a Child* will come out. Go to our website for a sample chapter. Beth's infertility and then car accident slammed her hopes for ever having a child. A new dream, like a whirlwind, sweeps her in a life or death search for the baby she's come to love.

Early in 2021, Barbara's YA book, *Prankster's Last Shot,* will come out. Jeremy's prank backfired and destroyed his family's lives and his own. His consequences are more than he can bare. How can he redeem himself? (Teach kids about consequences.)

If you'd like to receive our newsletter with monthly updates and freebies, send your email to barbararicewrites@gmail.com.

[1] "Idiot Light," by Dave McClellan, Crosspoint, January/February 2001 www.crosspointscripts.com used by permission.
[2] John M. Gottman Ph.D. *Why Marriages Succeed or Fail and How You Can Make Yours Last.* New York, NY: Firestone, 1994, page 57.
[3] Neil Clark Warren, *Date . . . or Soul Mate? How to Know If Someone Is Worth Pursuing in Two Dates or Less* (Nashville, TN: Thomas Nelson) 191.
[4] Neil Clark Warren, *Date . . . or Soul Mate? How to know if Someone Is Worth Pursuing in Two Dates or Less,* (Nashville, TN: Thomas Nelson, 2002) 176.
[5] Samantha Gallo, Blog Post: *The Effect of Pornography on Families,* January 7, 2019, Human Defense Initiative, https://humandefense.com/the-effect-of-pornography-on-families/.
[6] Sheri Stritof, *The Spruce,* -(thespruce.com/cohabitation-facts-and-statistics, updated 08/14/19).

Made in United States
Troutdale, OR
10/11/2023